God-Sized Dreams

God-Sized Dreams

The story of a little black girl from the South Side of Chicago

Debra Williamson

November Media Publishing, Chicago IL.

Ordering Information: Special discounts are available on quantity purchases by corporations, associations, and others. For details, contact the publisher at the email address above.

Printed in the United States of America

ISBN: 978-0-9990431-3-4

Editing: November Media Publishing

Cover Design: Danielle Truckenmiller

Interior Design: November Media Publishing

TO GOD, THE ARCHITECT OF MY DREAMS; IF I HAD 10,000 TONGUES.......

This book is dedicated to the true North of my life, my husband, best friend, the lover of my soul, the lifter of my spirit, the light in my darkness, my safe place & my king, Derek. Thank you for giving me the freedom to be different, make mistakes, be candid and most of all vulnerable. You made me uncomfortable; you made me write this book. I'm glad you did and I'm forever grateful. I love you!

This book is dedicated to my miracle, my 'mini-me,' Jordyn. It's my honor to be your mother. You fill my heart with unspeakable joy. My life had no meaning until the day you were born. Thank you for unselfishly allowing me to give myself to the world. Where ever you may go in life, Jordyn, my love goes with you.

This book is dedicated to my father & mother and all of my siblings. Because of your love, support and encouragement over the years, I was able to let God size my dreams. The power of family is a force multiplier. I love you all dearly. I miss you daddy and Wendell!

This book is dedicated to the sisterhood – to every child, girl or woman who has ever doubted her existence or questioned her value; you are enough and your enoughness is awesome!

CONTENTS

FOREWORD

Debra Williamson is the personification of wisdom. Much like her namesake in the Bible, God set her apart to impart wisdom into the lives He ordained for her to touch. I am privileged to be one of those lives. I am honored to call her my friend and partner in ministry.

When Debra told me she was writing a book, I was so excited for her, because I knew it was what God had purposed for her to long before she ever felt the call to write. Now, she would tell you she feels like the most unlikely person to be writing a book such as this because of her background and life struggles. But I beg to differ. I wholeheartedly believe God ordained her steps along the way to prepare for "such a time as this."

When something is birthed out of pain and comes from the most unlikely place, to impart hope into lives, that's when God gets the glory! That is why I truly believe *God-Sized Dreams: The Story of a*

Little Black Girl from the Southside of Chicago is an anointed and appointed book.

I encourage you to allow the words that will spill out on the pages of this book to pour into your spirit. May they encourage, inspire, provoke, and push you to a place where you will allow God to open the closed off places, where you refuse to let anyone in. This book will resonate with more people than Debra could ever imagined it would. I know this because she is writing it from a fully vulnerable and transparent place. My prayer is that you would feel a connection to her story and know you are not alone. I want you to know that, if God can use a little black girl from the South Side of Chicago to reach and impact lives, He has also chosen to use you. You only have to say YES and then prepare to let God, the chief dreamer, dream a God-Sized dream for you!

Rose M. Chavez
Co-Pastor - Phoenix World Outreach
Co-Founder - Marriage Tool-Belt Ministries
Author, *Desperate Pastors' Wives*

PROLOGUE

"Either write something worth reading or do something worth writing."

-Benjamin Franklin

Truth. Let's start here. Sojourner Truth said, "Truth is powerful, and it prevails." I know what it is to live a lie — to want a relationship so badly that you create an alternate ego just to impress a man. I know what it's like to walk in the darkness of lies to the point of exhaustion. I know what it's like to immerse oneself in spiritually unhealthy behaviors that only produce more lies. I know what it's like to engross yourself in work and other distractions, so you don't have to face the truth. I've experienced disappointment. I know what it's like to make a right choice, which produced a horrific outcome.

I am pregnant. How can this be? I am only 18. I vividly remember my mother and father's disappointment in me when they learned the news. The looks on their faces ripped my heart out. How could I have disappointed the only two people in the world who had ever actually loved *me* and did everything they could to give me a 'perfect' life?

My father was *sooo* angry with me. I believe his anger was more so grief. He told me that he would pay for my abortion and drive me to the abortion clinic if I would just do it. "Let's go, he said sternly." He told me that this baby would ruin my life and I'd likely end up on welfare. He said that my baby's father was a bum and that he would never work or be able to take care of me.

He assured me my future would not be bright and I would not amount to anything. I have never been so scared in my entire life.

Growing up, I always had this sixth sense that I was 'special,' not in a mentally challenged way, but in a way that made me feel like I was going to become something great. Eighteen, single and pregnant is not the way to greatness. I realized that this was my defining moment and that what I would decide next would forever change my life.

On April 17, 1979, at 8:00 pm, the pain was excruciating. Unlike anything I've ever experienced. There was profuse vaginal bleeding and projectile vomiting. My abdomen was harder than a bowling ball, and I could hardly breathe. I was barely conscious but miraculously managed to call 911. Racing through the halls of the emergency room, I heard the doctors scream, "We're losing her. Get her to OR stat!"

It's 6:30 am, April 18, 1979. "Debra, do you know where you are?" No answer. The nurse asked again, "Debra, do you know where you are?" In an anesthetized haze, I grumbled, "What happened?" The nurse replied, "You're in the recovery room. You had emergency surgery." Almost faintly, I groaned, "Where's my baby?" The nurse replied abruptly, "Your baby is dead!"

"What?" "Not possible!" Unable to articulate the range of emotions, confusion, and pain I was feeling, that's all I could say.

How could God do this to me? I **made** a good choice, the **best** option. I chose to defy my father and take responsibility for the life I created; a baby boy that I carried to full term. How does a baby die after 9-months? This is crazy! Maybe my father's admonishment to me foretold this event; that having this child would ruin my life. Then, out of nowhere, I heard an audible voice say, ***"Debra,*** *look for purpose in your pain."* Was this the voice of God or was I hallucinating?

Maybe it's true what some people say that who you are is just a collection of choices; decisions that somehow all add up to the person you become. I used to think that your choices either made you good or bad; responsible or irresponsible, but maybe that's not quite right, perhaps it's more like your choices either make your more or make you less, *yourself;* who you are, who you were always meant to be.

Even with the best plans, we never see many things that happen in life. We all encounter things in life (to some degree) that aren't *supposed* to happen. Whether it's a consequence of something we've done, or simply circumstances out of our control.

Before I was discharged from the hospital, the doctors told me that I had experienced a severe, unpredictable case of "Placenta Abrutia" and that I was lucky to be alive. This is a condition where the placenta, which is the organ that supplies food and oxygen to the baby during pregnancy, detaches from

4

the wall of the womb (uterus) before delivery. The cause is unknown.

Plans change, and sometimes they disappear. Most of our plans don't allow for second chances, but God does. Life happens but God is still there.

"When I discover who I am, I'll be free," the great novelist, Ralph Ellison said. All I wanted in life was simple: the freedom to build a professional career and become a successful, powerful, influential black woman. These days, they call it being a "Boss Lady!"

I wanted the house, the car, the designer clothes, and expensive jewelry. I wanted it all. Now, this may seem shallow to some, but these were my priorities. This *was* my truth.

I'm different today. God's truth is the glue that holds my life together. Walking in truth has radically changed the landscape of my life. I have a covenant with the truth. This truth guides me, supports me and connects me no matter how difficult the road or how long the journey. God's truth gave me life.

This book is intended for a tapestry of girls of all shades, races, shapes, sizes, professions, and ages.

This book is to spare the pain of every woman who fears that she can have love only if she erases herself.

My hope is this book will encourage you to not see yourself as a failure in relationships, and not to feel unworthy of the love of a godly man. Notice I said a godly man and not a good man. There is a difference. I was afraid to look at the junk in my life. I've written this book to tell you that you can be driven by your dreams and your passions. Your passion will be revealed to you when you figure out what you stand for.

I've written this book to tell you your mistakes are just that, mistakes… a moment in time. When mistakes happen, it's how you react that counts.

I've written this book to encourage you in the face of trials, storms, tests, and uncertainty — when tragedy happens, and the winds and waves consume us, God is in the midst.

I've written this book to tell you it's not about what you do, but rather who you are and who you want to become. I've written this book to tell you everything you want is on the other side of fear.

A dream doesn't drive you; it draws you. It is like a big magnet that pulls you toward itself. That dream in your heart contains your spiritual "DNA" the blueprint for who you are. Your dream is that idea that vision for your life that burns inside of you— something you can't ignore for long. It keeps coming back to your mind because it is part of who you are; it will never leave you alone.

I've written this book to tell you God is a dreamer! This book is your invitation to dream God-sized dreams. When we attempt to dream the dreams, God has established for us; powerful things take place. God's dream is always bigger than us! I must. You must. We must dream God-sized dreams.

INTRODUCTION

"Faith is acting like it is so, even when it's not so so that it might be so, only because God said so."

— Priscilla Shirer

Today is April 23, 2014, and it's 10:45 in the morning. Here I am, standing in front of a room filled with beautiful women of God, full of life, joy, and purpose. They are here because they thirst for the word of God. I was overjoyed when I was asked to speak to this elite group. "Why me?" I thought. What I didn't realize was that this day and this message was, in fact, a part of my destiny — God's destiny for me!

I'm prepared to teach at a women's Bible study on the topic, *Living the Dream*, I chuckled under my breath. The first thought I had when I was asked to teach on this subject was, *"Am I living my dream?"*

In fact, I began to think much deeper and asked myself, *"Am I living my dream or am I living someone else's dream?"* This made me self-reflect.

Imagine for a moment that Jesus said we would do even greater works than he did. It's not imaginary, he said it. "I tell you the truth, anyone

8

who believes in me will do the same works I have done, and even greater works, because I am going to be with the Father (John 14:12, The New Living Translation (NLT)).

"Now, I don't know about you, but the idea of me being able to do the same things Jesus did and even greater seems impossible."

This truth has taken me a lifetime to understand. The enemy wants to deceive us by attacking our identity in Christ by influencing how we think and how we see ourselves.

As I cleared my throat, I glanced over the room once again. I was a little nervous, to say the least. I don't like public speaking, and by nature, I am timid. I had to rely on my faith!

I had my notes written on several pieces of paper in front of me. This compilation of paper represented a good portion of my life. I exhaled, as I thought, "This was a tough message to prepare.

How on earth could I tell these women of God if they were "Living The Dream?" How was I supposed to teach a message that required complete transparency? Don't ask me why, because you all know that when you put yourself out there, you invite others in to criticize and make judgments about you.

However, in my heart,

"I knew it was time to share my story. We all have an important story to tell. Every event in your life, every choice you made has brought you to this point in your life."

In fact, God in all His sovereignty pre-destined this moment for me, a little black girl from the Southside of Chicago.

WHY DOES GOD GIVE US DREAMS?

An entire nation shook under the power of one man's [MLK's] dream! Now if one dream can do that for our nation, imagine what a dream can do for the Kingdom of God.
–Wayne Cordeiro

A wise person once explained the importance of dreams in this way:

"Dreams are the perfect way to hear from God. When you are dreaming, you are quiet, so you can't ignore Him. Plus, you are not easily distracted. You're all ears for about seven hours every night."

The Bible confirms it this way: "For God speaks again and again, though people do not recognize it. He speaks in dreams, in visions of the night, when deep sleep falls on people as they lie in their beds. He whispers in their ears," (Job 33:14-16, NLT). It is His way of speaking directly to us.

I wondered, "If this is the way God directs our path? How do you know if the dreams you have come from God? How can you tell if it's just not something you thought up yourself?"

The Bible says in Ephesians 3:20, "That God by his mighty power working within us is able to do far more than we would ever dare to ask or even dream of infinitely beyond our highest prayers, desires,

11

thoughts, or hopes The New International Version (NIV).

"I think that if a dream comes from God, it will be so big in your life you cannot accomplish it by your own strength. If you could, then you wouldn't need faith, and if you do not have faith, then you are not pleasing God, because the bible tells us, "without faith, it's impossible to please God," (Hebrews 11:6 (NIV))."

Without further hesitation, I closed my eyes to prepare my mind and heart for prayer. I needed God to decrease me and increase His presence. I needed Him to guide my words, to calm my spirit, and to use me like He did every single time I asked Him.

I smiled as a warm feeling of peace and love filled my soul. *I was His vessel,* and knowing this was the greatest comfort in the world for someone who struggled half of her life to be in control. This morning I stood here empty before the Lord, and ready to do His will! I began to pray:

'Father God, we thank you for the opportunity to come before you to surrender it all. We are grateful to you, Lord, that you are the God who gives us our dreams. I ask that you would bless every woman here today. Father, as I teach I pray that every word would resonate with these women's spirits and anything that I say that is not a reflection of the pureness of your heart, you wash it away with the precious blood of Jesus. Amen.'

So, I said, "Ladies, let's get to work!"

CHAPTER ONE:

HAPPILY, EVER AFTER......
IS THERE SUCH A THING?

"Always remember that your outlook determines your outcome."

-Bishop Dale Bronner

Most of us (women) in particular, get married with the dream of living happily ever after, but in between the marriage and the happily ever after, life happens!

"Life is a cruel teacher; she often gives us the test before she ever provides us with the lesson."

My life's tests were inconceivable. Thank God, my lessons were not far behind. I navigated my adult life thinking that marriage and relationships were a waste of time. Now, don't get me wrong, my thinking at the ripe old age of 25 was that if you were married and had a good marriage, then good

14

for you! My outlook lined up with my experiences and my expectations.

Most of the women I knew that were in relationships (married or single) were just like me, melting away in a noxious wasteland. The one thing that separated me from these other poor souls was that to my benefit, I was raised to be a man, not physically but literally. I know this sounds strange, but my father taught me how to take care of myself and not rely on any man for ANYTHING; provision, love, protection, or money. As far as my father was concerned, no man would ever be good enough.

My father instilled in me an audacious sense of self-reliance. Daddy taught me "if a man could not do more for me than I could do for myself, I didn't need him." I remember when I was sixteen, my father told me that all a man wanted to do was "stick something in me and fill me full of infection." Yes, he said that and this became ingrained into my BS (belief system). Nasty! How gross, "I never wanted to be infected."

The equation was simple: sex = infection.

"I can remember not having the desire to be married. Frankly, I hated marriage and the idea of marriage because of what I saw my parents go through."

I was sure that marriage was not for me.

Since I'm walking in truth, I have a confession to make. I've been married before, twice; does this fact shatter your illusion? My first experience with marriage was when I was 18 and pregnant with the boy who 'knocked me up.'

My father should have been a prophet. He was spot-on in every way when we had that painful conversation in the basement, you know the one, (when he offered to pay for my abortion), and he informed me that my life was headed for total and complete ruin.

At that time, the only thing that seemed to make sense and make all of the hurt and disappointment I caused my parents go away, was to get married. Imagine doing the right thing for the wrong reason.

16

I had a 'ghetto fabulous' wedding. I got married in my prom dress from the year before in the upper peninsula of Michigan at a cabin in the woods. It was nothing romantic, nothing memorable, just necessary.

Although he agreed to the marriage, I knew he didn't love me, wouldn't keep a job, and couldn't provide for me. Even after all of that, I fought for this marriage and my son. I HAD to prove my father wrong but I couldn't. Daddy *was* right on every level. I didn't see it then, but I certainly see it now.

After we married, I remember feeling that we'd never have anything and I **could not** be destitute. My husband could not put a roof over my head (daddy prophesy #1). After I was able to find an apartment for us to live in, we moved in and had no furniture. Out of pride and shame, I didn't have good enough credit to buy furniture, so I did the next best thing and rented furniture from a company called "Swingles." Yes, I rented furniture. I had to keep up appearances. Besides, the man I

17

married couldn't rub two cents together to make a penny (daddy prophesy #2)!

The shame and embarrassment of being pregnant, now married and not being able to live normally took its toll on me emotionally. By the way, it didn't take long for Swingles to repossess my rented furniture.

When I replay this season of my life, I couldn't help but think that it was stress like this (and so many other stressful events which included riding the bus while standing up, 60 miles each day, pregnant, so my husband could use my car *to not* look for a job – daddy prophesy #3) may have caused the stillbirth of my son.

My life was in ruins (daddy prophesy #4). I needed to believe that all of this was happening to me for a reason, something needed to make sense.

"I knew this marriage was a mistake the moment I put my prom dress on and passed it off as a wedding gown. My "15-minute" marriage crumbled under the weight of

ignorance, ill preparedness, immaturity, and a foundation built on sand."

After we divorced, I could feel that a metamorphosis was occurring. I was done fighting trying to prove I was worthy and good enough for a decent man or a healthy relationship.

THE UPSIDE OF GIVING UP

"When things go wrong, don't go with them."
—Elvis Presley

Do you know the story of the man who was hitting himself over the head with a hammer? "Why do you keep hitting yourself with that hammer?" A shocked passerby asked him. "Because," the man replied, "it's going to feel so good when I stop."

Examine the evidence. You keep fighting the same fight. You're losing sleep. You're sick of hearing yourself complain about the same things over and over again. Then you realize that …you have no fight left in you.

I had no more fight left in me, so I stopped fighting. I had to start dreaming. I had entirely abandoned my dreams, which led to the death of a child, divorce, and heartbreak.

I decided that I was going to stop fighting with this circus called my life because I just wanted peace. I'm going to stop grinding for the wrong things because I want more ease in my life. I'm declaring my debt to karma PAID, IN FULL!

I was done learning my lessons through suffering; I was going to learn more gracefully now.

"I learned that you find truth when you are strong, and you have strength when you have the truth."

Truth: I will have my "happily ever after" even if I have to buy it myself!

CHAPTER TWO:

LITTLE BLACK GIRL FROM THE SOUTHSIDE

"One shall be born from small beginnings which will rapidly become vast. This will respect no created thing, rather will it, by its power, transform almost everything from its own nature into another."

-Leonardo da Vinci

I was born at Presbyterian St. Luke's Hospital (now known as Rush Medical Center) on the Westside of Chicago on September 12, 19xx (a lady never tells her age!) I am the third of six children. Initially, growing up there were only four children— my two brothers, my sister and me. My two younger sisters were born after my sophomore year in high school.

My family lived briefly in the North Lawndale area in Chicago known as *K-Town*. After my third or fourth birthday, we moved to a Southside community called Morgan Park. Our home was a brand-new build. I remember my mother telling me I was her good luck charm because after we moved

21

into our new home, daddy bought her a washer and dryer.

Our neighborhood had a community park with a swimming pool, and we had great neighbors. Because our community was safe, we left our front doors opened and unlocked. We played outside and made up games to amuse ourselves. Whenever the streetlights came on, this was our signal that it was time to get inside.

My brothers were ordinary boys: one older and one younger. My older brother teased me relentlessly. My little brother was a pain; he was always getting into trouble! My older sister was a glamor girl, and I lived in her shadow. She was so beautiful. Back in those days, there was a song by the Commodores, "She's a Brick House" that was my sister all the way. She was beautiful, and I wanted more than anything to look like and be like her. All the boys loved her and she didn't even have to try to impress. Her confidence fell off her in waves, and she knew she had it *goin'* on, and she embraced it!

I remember sometimes looking at her and thinking, "Oh my God, what do I have to do to make a boy look at me like that?" But no matter what I did — and I'm sure I did some crazy things — they still never paid me any attention.

"I don't know any young girl, who would admit she's not cute enough. After a while, I gave up, and I did my best to develop my own interests. I loved reading the dictionary, I figured if I can't have beauty then at least I can have brains!"

I attended Catholic schools from kindergarten through and including the twelfth grade. During my childhood, I wanted to become a nun. In their stately, black robes and covered heads, nuns appeared to be powerful, poised, and perfect — the trifecta for getting into heaven.

The church and the community respected them. Nuns, to me, had a purpose and a sense of belonging, which is something I longed for in my younger years.

Sr. Dolorosa was my favorite nun. She was always kind, and she inspired me to learn. I always thought she was firm but fair — the opposite of Sr. DeLasalle, the school principal. I was the 'teacher's pet' because Sr. Dolorosa always asked me to be class monitor and hall monitor; jobs that I gladly accepted.

According to Sr. DeLasalle, black hairstyles such as the afro or cornrowed braids made us look like heathens, so we weren't allowed to wear our hair like that to school.

Sr. DeLasalle also had this weird 'twitch', which made her appear meaner than she was. You never knew when she would be ready to snap. If she started 'twitching' quickly, you better take cover; someone was about to catch a case. She was not afraid of corporal punishment. You could always find her cracking some poor kid's knuckles with the side of her ruler.

TEN HAIL MARY'S, ONE ACT OF CONTRITION AND THE LORD'S PRAYER.

"Guilt: the gift that keeps on giving!"
—Erma Bombeck

I went to mass six times a week: every day before school and on Sunday. I went to confession weekly each Saturday. I couldn't wait to shed my guilt and shame. I walked down the street to Holy Name of Mary Church. Confessions began at 4 p.m.

It felt good to have a priest sit in a box, speak to me in an ominous tone, and listen to and forgive me of my sins. I vividly remember one time I entered the confession box. The side shutter slid open. I confessed my shame, and prayed Fr. Vader wouldn't probe. After I finished confessing my sins, Fr. Vader asked me if I took cold baths. I said no. He advised me I should. He asked me if I slept with the window open. I stated that I did in the summer. He encouraged me to include winter, spring, and fall. He asked me if I ran around the block. I said only if somebody was chasing me. He suggested I take up running. My penance was 10 Hail Mary's, 1 Act of Contrition and the Lord's Prayer.

Absolved of my sins, I crept out of the box, said 10 Hail Mary's, 1 Act of Contrition and the Lord's Prayer, and walked back home. Later that night I took a cold bath, I ran around the block, and I slept with the window wide open. The next morning, I woke up with a terrible cold, but it was all worth it.

The cool thing after confession is that I could commit another sin and have more guilt, which led to more fear, shame, and sin. I'd go back in the box to confess and voila! My sins would all disappear — only for me to start the process all over again the next week. What a vicious cycle but to me, there was only one *true* religion; and that was Catholicism.

On Sundays, my parents sent us to mass. I remember sitting there week after week, dutifully listening to Fr. Vader going on and on about how we were all going to go to hell if we didn't obey the laws and the rules of the Catholic Church.

Each Sunday, my siblings and I sat on the hard pews on our best behavior. We knew better than to act up in church. Honestly speaking, we feared the wrath of God and his nuns. I was so afraid of God.

"Looking back, I now see I did not have a personal relationship with God — at least that's how it felt. I had an unhealthy fear of God; the kind of fear that creates guilt and shame. I learned all about the consequences of doing wrong and not enough about his love, grace and our need for salvation."

For the longest, I believed if you were bad, or did something wrong then all you had to do was go to confession, say your 'Hail Mary's' and be on your way.

I am not sure what type of effect this had on my siblings. However, I believe this was the beginning of my obsession with perfectionism. For me, perfection had less to do with me wanting to be great and more to do with me fearing the results of not achieving greatness.

SMALL BEGINNINGS

Do not despise these small beginnings, for the Lord rejoices to

see the work begin, to see the plumb line in Zerubbabel's hand."
-Zechariah 4:10 (NLT)

My parents were hard workers. My father was a career Chicago police officer, while my mother was a career civil servant, who worked at the post office. They were both raised in the South, Tennessee, and Mississippi, respectively. They had strong family and Christian values. My father's dad was a pastor at St. Paul CME Church in Jackson, Tennessee. I suspect this is why my dad never went to church. You know the reputation PK's (preacher's kids) get!

My childhood was ideal. Our home was very stable growing up; I had two parents that seemingly loved one another other, and we lived very comfortably.

My parents ensured we had everything we needed. They believed in education and the opportunities a good education would provide. My mother changed her religious affiliation from Baptist to Catholic so we could attend private Catholic schools; that was the only way we could be admitted.

My father worked two jobs to make sure our tuition was paid. My parents wanted to give us advantages in life they never had. My dad became obsessed with the appearance that we had wealth. He was the first person in our neighborhood to own a Cadillac Fleetwood Brougham. Back in the day that was a big deal and daddy had the first "hog" on the block! He would lavish my mother with extravagant gifts such as a Chinchilla coat and a 4-carat ruby ring, mom's birthstone.

My mother had our home professionally decorated by an interior designer from a high-end furniture store. We took family vacations, and we were members of the Millionaire's Club. Life was better than good; you could say it was *happily ever after*.

Then the unthinkable happened! Mom got pregnant when I was sixteen (a sophomore in high school). I can't tell you the embarrassment I felt! The bottom dropped out of my world; the thought of my parents having sex was gross! After the birth of my baby sister, three years later mom was pregnant again! Good grief! Stop having sex! Shortly after the birth of my little sister, I could tell my mom and dad's relationship was strained because of all the arguments they were having.

What seemed inevitable became evitable – mom and dad got divorced after 21 years of marriage and six kids later. No more *happily ever after!* My world was shattered. How can two people who seemed to be happy end up utterly miserable? Were they living a lie?

My parent's divorce created a new standard for me that shattered my illusions about marriage. My new normal was that marriage did not work, period. If you have problems, you don't work them out. You either leave or you turn to someone else for comfort.

LIFE AS I KNEW IT

"What could I say to you that would be of value, except that perhaps you seek too much, that as a result of your seeking you cannot find?" –Herman Hesse

I've always been proud of my roots. Chicago gets a bad reputation nowadays, but growing up my parents made sure we had the best that life could give. As I said, my mother worked at the post office, and my father was a Chicago police officer. The way police officers conduct themselves today and the negative way the media portrays their roles, makes me wish I had told my father how proud I was of him and how honorably he served our city. He always wore his badge with pride and acted with integrity. I think a lot of police officers could learn a thing or two from him today.

Grammar school ignited my desire to learn.

"I wasn't sporty or athletic, but I excelled in academics; reading, writing, and math were no match for me. I prided myself on every academic accomplishment, no matter how small it was."

My biggest accomplishment (aside from being a teacher's pet and hallway monitor) was being voted

31

the class president in eighth grade. I had to prepare the commencement speech for graduation. My father worked tirelessly with me on this speech, because daddy told me that I had to *knock it out of the park* and thanks to him, I did.

After graduating elementary school, my sister and I were sent to an elite, all-girl college preparatory high school; Elizabeth Seton, in the suburb of South Holland, Illinois. This school cost my parents a lot of money, but it was the best private all-girl Catholic school in the state.

Every morning our father would take my sister and me to our bus stop, where we would then take a 45-minute trip on a big yellow school bus for the long ride to school.

I was an excellent student, smart and gifted, yet incredibly shy. I could outsmart anybody on any day, but deep down, I was unsure about so many things concerning myself and I had zero confidence.

People underestimate the effects of having low self-esteem. You can't do anything well in good conscious because there's always a little nagging voice in your head questioning you and making you feel so small.

I remember spending hours and hours playing the board game, Monopoly with my best friend. When I wasn't doing that, I daydreamed of being an inventor. I would tinker around with gadgets and knick-knacks, and when that wasn't entertaining enough, you would often find me reading the dictionary or the encyclopedia.

Most little girls I knew didn't engage in those types of activities back then, but that was my norm. In fact, my big brother and his friends wanted to make it clear to me that this was *abnormal.* They would tease me for it; they even gave me the nickname, *Dictionary.* This was not a compliment, but rather a *dig* to how nerdy they thought I was.

According to my big brother, I was "skinny as a racehorse," and I looked like Diana Ross! Ughhh, thin with big eyes; not a good look. Kids can be so cruel— a lesson I learned quickly as a child.

I was so desperate to fit in. I wanted to fit in with all the other popular kids and be as beautiful as my sister... and Lord knows I didn't want to be known as *Dictionary*!

This began to take a mental and emotional toll on me, and made me desire more and more and to be something I wasn't. I felt I was dealt a crappy hand in life. Why wasn't I beautiful? Why wasn't I cool? Everything seemed to come so easy for everyone else around me. These feelings did nothing but feed my spirit of rejection. I needed to be someone else!

"I didn't realize that the things that make you strange are the same things that make you powerful."

Every day I remember waking up and hoping this was all a dream and that my life was in fact just the way I wanted it. I remember at different points in my childhood, and even through adolescence, I wanted all the wrong things for all the wrong reasons. I was a seeker who looked for happiness and different ways to become a better person. I searched for a new life that would be as perfect as the lives I saw my friends living.

CHAPTER THREE:

MY DREAM IS CALLING...
OR SO I THOUGHT!

"You go through the faith-phases of Dream, Decision, Delay, Difficulty, and Dead End, and then comes Deliverance."

-Rick Warren

School auditoriums were always so hot in the spring and summer. I watched my older brother and sister graduate high school and move on in life; now it was my turn to wear the white robe of distinction and change my tassel from right to left. Through the sea of faces, I could see my family in the stands, as they watched the ceremony.

"I knew my parents were proud of me. They didn't work hard to have an easy life, but they worked hard to give my siblings and I the best chance to succeed in life, and become successful adults. I wanted to be something great."

I wanted my dream job and my ideal life. I wanted to look back on my life twenty or thirty years from then and be content in knowing I made the right choices at the right time and the choices that were best for me.

As we prepared to march in for graduation, I heard the side conversations of my fellow graduates discussing their post-high school plans — college primarily. I was happy for them. I hoped they got all they wanted to get out of life.

When they called my name, I held my head high, as I walked up to the stage to accept my diploma. I could hear my family going crazy in the stands cheering for me and clapping. It's crazy how a piece of paper may determine how far you go in life.

After graduation, my dream was to enter the workforce. I decided **not** to go to college like my friends and classmates. You can imagine how unhappy my parents — the same ones who sent me to the best schools my entire life — felt about this decision. Just like I had a vision for my life, so did they.

If I had made different choices, I probably would have gone to one of the better colleges, continued to medical school and started a private medical practice. Those aspirations sounded nice, but I just couldn't find it in myself to travel this path. I felt the universe had something different for me and I was sure that I could just go out into this massive world on my own and take my fate into my own hands and make *my* dreams come true.

Realizing he wouldn't be able to change my mind, my father said to me, "Well, if this is your choice, Little Deb, then I'll tell you what, if you're going to work, the best thing you could do is get a "good government job." According to my dad, government jobs paid well, I would receive great benefits and keep this job for the rest of my life. He was right, again!

Armed with this knowledge and this new perspective, I took the Federal Civil Service Examination and scored a 99%; just because I didn't want to go to school anymore didn't mean I wouldn't do my absolute best on an exam.

WORKING NINE TO FIVE & MOVING ON UP!

"I love to see a young girl go out and grab the world by the lapels. Life's a bitch. You've got to go out and kick ass."
– Maya Angelou

Nothing can dim the light that shines from within."
–Maya Angelou

My first official "real" job was at the Treasury Department. I worked as a GS-2 File-Clerk with an annual salary of $6,000. Yes, you read that right. I was making $6,000 a year performing tasks in the most mundane job on the planet. Just to give you an idea, if you've ever received a government issued check — paychecks, IRS refund checks, or social security retirement checks, for example, you might have noticed the 16-digit number in the right-hand corner.

If you can't relate, imagine this, my job was to stand in a barren, industrial room filled with file cabinets taller than me and file those checks in numeric sequence, all 16 digits in order! This was my entrance into the workforce. I'm living my dream, or so I thought. I performed this mundane task every single day for 39 hours a week. Very glamorous, right? Not!

Believe me when I tell you it didn't take long for me to realize this was not going to work for me. I didn't forgo college to wind up doing menial tasks, and I couldn't make this a long-term job. I set my sights on a higher goal: a desk job.

I thought to have a nice desk was a status symbol that any career oriented person had made it to the big league. Only important people with serious jobs have desks. You don't get a desk for filing checks in numerical order all day. I was determined to work my way up and achieve this sought-after status symbol.

"This is when I finally realized there were three things you could do with time: waste it, spend it or invest it. I decided I would invest my time."

I took my little entry-level job, and I filed those checks day in and day out; this whet my appetite and gave me a taste of where motivation and determination can lead you.

I persisted and put in for a promotion for that coveted desk job. Not to my surprise, I was selected for that position. On the first day of my new job, when I sat down, I realized I still wasn't satisfied. In the building where I worked, the people on the eighth floor had offices. Guess what I wanted next? If I were lucky, my new office would even have a window.

Now I have a new dream. I'm going up to the eighth floor to get my office. As fate would have it, I did not get an office on the eighth floor; something happened much better than that. A friend informed me the VA was hiring. I was intrigued by the possibilities, so I set my sights on this new opportunity.

I applied for and was hired to be the secretary to the medical center Chaplain. By this time, I was a GS-4, and you couldn't tell me anything. It wasn't my dream job, but I figured I was ahead of everyone else. In my opinion, I was on my way, and I scored that office.

Still operating in my own strength and living out what I thought was my dream, I took that job, and I worked it like no one else could. I slayed! I went to work early and stayed late. I impressed the people that needed to be impressed.

"My determination was only secondary to my determination!"

I zealously put in for promotion after promotion. I remember thinking, "This is really good."

I guess I was hooked at that point. Every time there was an opportunity for me to apply for a higher-level job, I did. I got a little taste of success, and I wanted more — more success, more authority, more money, more everything until I finally realized that I had gotten everything I could out of the Windy City.

In my eyes, I was too big for Chicago. I wondered how I could have ever had that mindset — I'm too big for anything or place. I know some people like to forget where they come from or what they went through, especially if they're not proud of whatever it was they were doing. However, one thing I learned is that every situation, every hurt, and every lesson learned is just another way of God bringing us closer to Him.

CHAPTER FOUR:

ALL THE THINGS I WISH I COULD FORGET

Nothing fixes a thing so intensely in the memory as the wish to forget it."

-Michel de Montaigne

I love being from Chicago. I'm a *Southside girl* through and through. Growing up for me and what made Chicago great were the hot summers, Ada Park, the Hoagie Shop on 111th Street, DiCola's Fish Market, Evergreen Plaza, Maxwell Street Jew-Town Polishes, the ridiculously cold winters, the Chicago Bears playing a home game at Soldier's Field, walking to school, and going to Mr. Brown's corner store to buy penny candy and cigarettes (with a permission note from our teenage neighbors.)

Whenever I had a little pocket change, on Friday nights I went roller-skating at the midnight ramble at Markham Roller Rink. That was my life, and I loved it.

I also loved our family vacations to Wisconsin Dells or driving to Jackson, Tennessee to visit my father's family and attend homecoming events at his alma mater, Lane College. I loved Christmas celebrations in our home. I loved our neighbors because they were more like family than friends. I loved the sense of society and self-identification of who I was, and how I was shaped and developed by my community. I loved the feeling of safety and security I experienced. Now as a young adult, I especially enjoyed the career I was building in Chicago.

The Bible says in 1 Corinthians 11:13 (NLT): "When I was a child, I talked like a child, I thought like a child, I reasoned like a child. When I became a man (*woman*), I put the ways of childhood behind me."

When I decided to leave the richness of my childhood experiences and my blooming career behind me,

"I set the wheels in motion to leave this life that I loved. It wasn't a decision I made lightly. However, my passion to keep climbing the

ladder of success quickly erased any hesitation from my thoughts," ...

and I ended up applying for a job at the San Diego VA Medical Center.

"This was a long-shot," I thought. "There's no way I would get selected for this position because I was the little black girl from the Southside of Chicago!" I quickly remembered a teaching from Bishop TD Jakes where he said, "We always prepare for the possibility of failure, but we never prepare for the possibility for success!"

I began to think, "I can do this. This is doable. I got this!" However, this revelation caused me to become nervous about the prospects of leaving the comfort and safety of the only placed I ever lived, Chicago. Several weeks later, after submitting my application, I received a letter in the mail that simply stated that I had been selected. Wow! Selected without so much as an interview. I couldn't help but think that this had to have been a big mistake. Truthfully though, I really didn't care if it was a mistake or not, it was too late. I accepted the position and packed up what little household belongings I possessed and boarded a plane heading towards San Diego, California!

This move was a tough transition for me. Now, I had to adjust to living and working in an unfamiliar environment; too many white people and not enough people of color. What's a black girl from the Southside of Chicago to do, ethnically speaking?

I worked hard to fit in; I even learned how to channel my inner California 'valley girl' persona. In my new position, I had to make a statement. I had to build credibility and the best way I felt that I could do this was to be a woman of integrity.

I impressed my new boss so much that it didn't take long before he chose me to serve as the Acting Assistant Chief, Medical Administration, while they were actively recruiting to fill the vacancy.

For four months as acting assistant chief, I did my best work. If there was a shortage of manpower in the departments, I managed. I became a worker bee and rolled up my sleeves and worked alongside the team so my staff met efficiency standards. Although I craved it, I never took credit when we passed our "Time Study" tests but rather gave credit to the team.

"This position was significantly more responsibility than I was accustomed to, but that didn't stop me from delivering more value than my boss could ever expect from me."

When the vacancy was officially announced, I thought I was a "shoo-in." I figured I'd go through the motions and submit my application for proper consideration to make this detail (a fancy government word for assigning you to do someone else's job without the pay), permanent.

WAKE UP CALL!

"Failure is the womb of success."
-Bishop Dale Bronner

With certitude, I eagerly awaited receipt of my selection letter. I checked my mailbox at work at least twice a day. Finally, the day that I had been waiting for, preparing for, planning for, arrived. I was anxious and a little nervous to open that envelope because I knew that my life was about to change. All of the odds were in my favor; there was **no way** I would not be selected for this position. The nervous tension was building. I closed my eyes and opened the letter.

When I opened my eyes, and read the letter, shockwaves traveled through every inch of my being as I noticed that the box on the form letter was checked, "Considered, but NOT SELECTED!" This had to be a mistake. Human Resources must have given my letter to someone else. I could feel my left lung collapsing. I was completely and utterly blindsided. Devastation doesn't even begin to describe the feelings I was processing. My devastation quickly turned to anger. I saw my entire dream evaporate like a snowflake hitting the ground when it's raining. In my mind, I was entitled to that position; I had worked harder than was required and I had proven myself, this job had *my name* on it. Why wouldn't Mr. Smith hire me after I broke my back proving to him I was the only viable choice?

The generic letter HR sent had no explanation for why I wasn't selected. However, I had to get some answers. So, I went to HR to find out why. The HR specialist told me that I needed to speak with the selecting official to get my questions answered.

Ok. I stormed my way to Mr. Smith's office, determined to get my answer. I asked his secretary if I could speak with him. She said, "Please wait a moment, Mr. Smith is extremely busy." I didn't care how busy he was. My life was in a total free-fall!

"While I waited, I used that time to calm down and collect my thoughts. I started to contemplate, "how do you ask someone why you weren't good enough?"

How do you challenge their decision? How do you settle with the results?" While I waited, I played this scenario in my mind, "Could you tell me why you didn't hire me? Because I'm awesome, and I can't figure out why you were so stupid as not to hire me. I mean, do you like a mediocre workforce? That can be the only reason why you didn't hire me."

I couldn't really say this, but honestly, that's exactly how I felt. I convinced myself this was all some perverse practical joke and Mr. Smith wanted to see me sweat. Frankly, that was the only explanation I was willing to accept.

Come to Jesus time! I woke up from daydreaming, and Mr. Smith's secretary motioned that he was ready to see me. I stood up from my seat and proceeded to take this excruciating long walk. Strangely, I felt like I was walking the *Green Mile*.

"Breathe, Debra, Breathe!"

Tap, tap, tap, I knocked on the door. "Mr. Smith, may I come in?"

"Yes, Debra," he replied. "Take a seat." With much trepidation, I sat down.

Do you know how hard it is to stand in righteous indignation and humility at the same time? In that split decision, I chose humility. I decided I needed to humbly ask for answers and be willing to accept the answers I was given.

I began, "Mr. Smith, I was stunned to learn that I was not selected for the position of Assistant Chief. I rambled for what felt like an eternity and never took a breath. I reminded him of my hard work, the positive changes I produced for the organization, how I boosted the morale of the department, I reminded him of the confidence he placed in me and how I delivered above and beyond his expectations, etcetera, etcetera, etcetera.

When he could get a word in edgewise, Mr. Smith, stated that while he appreciated my contributions to the service and my hard work, he simply wanted to fill his vacancy with someone who possessed a college degree! Immediately, there was a blanket of uncomfortable silence.

"This was the sum of all the things I wished I could forget!"

"College education?" I repeated, silently. You'd think the four months I spent performing ALL of the duties of the position, would make him want to hire me but at the end of the day, none of that mattered.

I was more than a little dramatic. I remember thinking, "Oh my God, my world is spiraling out of control; this could not possibly be happening!"

All my life my parents wanted the best for me. With my grades, I could have gone to a great college, but my decision not to go to college out of high school had finally come back to bite me where it hurts the most: my self-esteem.

I had a plan, or so I thought. I was living my dreams, or so I thought. I felt that God let me down by taking me all the way across the country, plucking me from my roots, my home, family, friends, and career in Chicago, by luring me to San Diego only to set me up to see me fail.

I guess that's man's default; blame God when we are unable and unwilling to accept responsibility for our own choices.

What I didn't understand then, was God had nothing to do with what was happening. This is what happens when you operate in your own will and don't leave room for God to work. The Word says in Jeremiah 29:11 (New Living Translation (NLT)), "For I know the plans I have for you, plans to prosper you and not to harm you, plans to give you hope and a future."

Hindsight is *always* 20/20. In hindsight, you can evaluate past choices more clearly than at the time of making that choice. This is precisely where I made a wrong choice.

How in the world do I process and accept this defeating blow and the tremendous sense of discouragement?

"The truth is that every man-made dream must pass the test of discouragement."

My first thoughts were, "Because of racism; I wasn't selected; because I was black." More importantly, I convinced myself I was not chosen because I was black *and* from the Southside of Chicago!

I could not accept the fact that I was not adequately prepared. This reality never entered my stream of consciousness. I felt used, hoodwinked, bamboozled, and led astray! I could not see the opportunity that I had been given; executive level experience, which I could use for my personal development.

Despite how difficult it was for me to face the facts about being rejected, I had to come to terms with the reality that my striving for prominence, acceptance, and placement clouded my ability to take responsibility for my life and own my choices. I allowed my flesh to take me to a place where my spirit could not operate in power. I meditated on my toxic emotions to the extent that I became emotionally wounded.

My broken heart led to my broken spirit. The Bible says in Proverbs 18:14 (NIV), "A man's spirit sustains him in sickness, but a crushed spirit who can bear?"

A wounded soul is an injury to any area of your mind, will, and emotions. This wound is an injury to the hidden areas of our three-part being. As the Word points out, a wounded spirit is worse than physical sickness. Physical sickness can be sustained by a healthy spirit that is in communion vertically with God, but a sick spirit cannot be sustained by anything. I felt as though all of my value and self-worth had been called into question. I began to live my life one-dimensionally; I could not find pleasure in anything. I was self-absorbed with my pain. I could not enjoy life at all. I was no benefit to anyone else. My spiritual hearing was crippled. I could not hear from God. I confused this with God being silent. These were the lies I told myself. My heart was closed to the fact that God was fully able to heal my spiritual and my emotional wounds.

The Bible says in Matthew 6:33 (King James Version (KJV), "But seek ye first the kingdom of God, and his righteousness; and all these things shall be added unto you." I had to seek God, period. This would be the only way I would gain any understanding.

Talk about the things I wished I could forget! This experience would be at the top of my list.

CHAPTER FIVE:

GOD DIGS CHICKS WITH SCARS!

"If you believe in the sovereignty of God, every wall becomes a gate!"

-Lisa Harper

Shortly after this crushing blow, I was left with a sense of hopelessness; I became filled with despair, anxiety and the spirit of rejection weighed heavily upon me. I'd been wounded and scarred in the past, and I know as long as we live, terrible things can happen that hurt us beyond our ability to recover, but this wound was different. This wound crippled me and left a big gaping scar.

Nonetheless, I persisted. I kept my head down, I continued to go to work, and I kept my problems to myself. By nature, I am a giver, it is in my blood, and is something I love to do, but I'm TERRIBLE at asking for help.

There was only one person that I could talk to who I knew would be able to empathize with me and talk me through this heart-wrenching disappointment. That person was my father.

"My father had the gift of 'effective persuasion.' he had a way about him that he could tell you that your baby was ugly and you wouldn't be offended."

My father reminded me to look at what I had achieved thus far. He told me not to count myself out; I wasn't out of the game. He recounted, "You're living in San Diego, California; a long way from the Southside of Chicago." My father said, "Lil Deb, you're just a little ol' black girl and what you're doing is unheard of!" What my father said reassured me and it made sense; I had accomplished a great deal in a short period. My meteoric rise was in no way finished. As long as I'm alive, I'm still in the game. There's a saying, "When something goes wrong in your life, just yell, 'plot twist!' and move on.

I'm a believer, and while I may have not always acted like a believer, one thing I knew was God promised He would neither leave me nor forsake me. I believed His promise.

Moving on, I was relegated to my previous position. My days seemed like weeks; weeks seemed like months; months felt like years. The humiliation I felt was soul crushing. Even through my father's encouragement, I continued to deceive myself that *race* had everything to do with being passed over for the job of a lifetime. My *pity party* had one guest: me!

I harbored resentment, and this was impacting my attitude. I knew deep down I needed to make a choice to change. Steve Maraboli said it this way,

"the truth is unless you let go, unless you forgive yourself and the situation, unless you realize that the situation is over, you cannot move forward."

I was convinced my opportunity was gone, but I had to move forward. Now I know blessings always come when you least expect them. I also know God can cause an opportunity to find you, and this is when He pours out those unexpected blessings.

Romans 8:28 says, "And we know that God causes everything to work together for the good to those who love God and are called according to His purpose for them" (NIV).

God has a way of shifting things in our favor. Looking back, I know this was God's way of saying, *"Get ready Debra, I'm about to shift things in your favor."*

THE SHIFT

"People of vision see the invisible, will hear the inaudible, will believe the incredible, and will think the unthinkable."
-Unknown

"Shift is acceleration. It will take you places you cannot get to on your own."

People with vision must see a world that does not yet exist. One morning, as I had my daily cup of coffee, a prominent pastor appeared on a television show speaking, ironically, about his new book, *Break Out!* Intrigued, I listened intently as he spoke. He said, "Doors will open for you that have not opened

60

in the past. Those who were against you will suddenly change their minds and be for you. Problems that have dogged you for years will suddenly turn around. You are coming into a shift. Because you have honored God, He will put you in a position you could never have attained on your own. It's not just your education, not just your talent, or the family you come from. It's the hand of God shifting you to a new level of your destiny." The pastor speaking was Joel Osteen. He continued, "Your new attitude should be: 'God, I'm ready. I'm taking the limits off of You. I'm enlarging my vision. I may not see a way, but I know You have a way. I declare I'm coming into a shift.'" This word was prophetic. It took me back to 1989.

Tuesday, January 10, 1989, the US president was **Ronald Reagan**. The most popular song at the top of the charts was **My Prerogative** by **Bobby Brown**. **Beaches**, directed by **Garry Marshall** was one of the most viewed movies released while **Clear and Present Danger** by **Tom Clancy** was one of the bestselling books. But something much more newsworthy happened on January 10, 1989.

Ring! *Ring*! *Ring*! The telephone on my desk blared. I was so busy I thought, "Let it go to voicemail." Impulsively, I answered the phone. The call was from the executive secretary of the medical center director. She relayed a request that Dr. Morrison wanted to meet with me.

I choked, "What in the world would he want to meet with me about? "How did he even know that I existed?" "Was I being called 'on the carpet' about my attitude?" No, that call would have come from my immediate supervisor, not the medical center director. "What in the world does this man want with me?" A million scenarios instantly played in my head, none of them good. Reluctantly, I accepted the meeting and decided to approach it with an open mind.

Dr. Morrison's office was impressive. It was filled with expensive furnishings, unlike anything I had ever seen. The walls were lined with mahogany bookcases that had more books than the public library. His desk, which looked like that of a US president, had neatly stacked files and what appeared to be important papers on top. The view of magnificent La Jolla, California from his expansive window was stunning.

I had a tough time catching my breath. Dr. Morrison invited me to take a seat. I made my way nervously to the chair across from his desk. It might as well have been the electric chair; because once I sat down I couldn't move. I sat stiffly in that chair as though I was strapped to it with my hands clasped in my lap, afraid to look too comfortable or fidget too much. I never felt that unsettled before in all my life. I went unconscious, not physically, but cognitively for sure. My mind went blank.

Dr. Morrison had a commanding presence. He was kind and engaging without being intimidating. There was a gentleness about him.

"He reminded me of Moses after his encounter with God at the burning bush, the image I remembered from watching the movie, *the ten commandments*."

Dr. Morrison's hair was white as snow and perfectly coiffed.

Although Dr. Morrison was a gentleman, he was no pushover. He was a man who had full command of his position and his authority. He shook my hand firmly and made me feel welcomed. Truthfully, I felt *like a fish out of water*. I think he could sense my uneasiness. To break the ice, Dr. Morrison simply asked me, "How are you doing, Debra?" I responded, "I'm fine, thank you for asking, Sir. How are you?" I stuttered. He said, "I'm fine as well, thanks." The awkwardness began to lift. Dr. Morrison asked me if I knew why he wanted to see me. I told him, "No, I had no idea." Then the real conversation began.

Dr. Morrison told me he had been observing me for some time and he was impressed with the work I performed while I was the acting, Assistant Chief, Medical Administration Service. He went on to say that during the time of my detail, he saw something in me – he qualified it as *great potential*. He further stated, "I watched how you carried yourself during high-pressure staff meetings, as well as the type of leader you are, and I was impressed with your professionalism and intelligence."

"Gushing, I thanked him for the recognition, but intuitively, I felt suspicious (that's the southside in me -- everyone had an agenda)."

My mind raced, and I couldn't help but think he knew **why** I had not been selected for that position on a permanent basis. I felt embarrassed and dove into self-talk. I created my own narrative around these questions: "Was I exposed?" The answer, "Yes!" "How did he know my dirty little secret?" The answer, "Human Resources told him!" "How did he know that I didn't have my degree?" The answer, "Mr. Smith told him!" "Was there a sign taped to my back that said, "Beware, she doesn't have a college degree?" The answer, "Yes, because I put the sign there!"

"If that was his angle, what was the end goal," I thought? One long shot I entertained was, "Maybe he's as outraged as I was by this injustice." Yeah, right, I must be dreaming!

After several minutes of small talk, Dr. Morrison went deeper and asked me about my plans and what

I wanted to do with my VA career. I didn't know how to answer him. Frankly, I felt like I was being set up, and that this question was a bit intrusive because I couldn't determine his motivation for inquiring.

With apprehension, I responded, "Well, ultimately, Dr. Morrison, my goal is to apply for the Associate Director training program." This goal *was* my ultimate dream.

The Associate Director Training Program is an upward, mobility training program that identifies, equips and trains a cadre of qualified individuals who possess the background and academic credentials needed to work in management roles in hospital administration. Upon successful completion of the training program, candidates are then selected to become hospital administrators.

If I could achieve this success, I'd be set professionally for life. This goal was my passion. This goal was the driving force behind me becoming a nomad, moving from city to city and job to job. I felt uneasy being this vulnerable and sharing my aspirations with Dr. Morrison because I didn't know what he'd think.

Wasting no time, Dr. Morrison straightforwardly responded, "Debra, that's an ambitious goal, and I know you are more than capable of accomplishing it, as well as taking on this level of responsibility. However, you do *know* you need to have a college degree to meet the minimum qualification standards, don't you?"

"That moment of absolute, unassailable truth sent me reeling. I was forced to acknowledge something I purposely chose to ignore."

That I, in fact, did need to get my college degree. Uncomfortable silence cloaked and lingered in his office like a fart in church. Talk about self-conscious, I felt so small, inferior, stupid, and filled with self-doubt.

Never, since my last Saturday afternoon confession in the confessional booth, had I felt more shame. My wounds were re-exposed. The

67

scab that had protected me all this time was picked off, and my scars were revealed for the world to see.

Have you ever seen the same commercial repeatedly? Or a movie, that when you see the trailer, you think, "I'll wait until this comes out on video!" You know it's advertising a great product, but for some reason, you just don't want to buy it.

That's how I felt. I was sick of hearing I needed a college degree. But this time was different, I felt the weight of the decision I made, at a time in my life where I was barely old enough to understand the consequences of my choice.

My mother used to tell me when I was sixteen, that she wished that everything in life that could have happened to me would have happened at sixteen because this was the age, according to my mother, that I thought I knew it all. I would have given anything to listen to my mom and dad's advice. Maybe if my head wasn't so hard...!

At that moment, I had to remind myself, "I made it this far. I'm capable. I'm qualified. I can do many things. Nothing can substitute experience,

68

which I had plenty of." My Bible tells me I can do
all things!

**"At that moment, I felt everything I worked
so hard for was toast — burnt toast. My passion,
my dream, was doused. I was hollow."**

What had I done and why had I been so
stubborn?

Anyone with ordinary sensibility should have
known *all* professionals had college degrees. I could
clearly hear my dream shatter like a mirror breaking
into a million pieces. Where in the world can this
conversation go now? It's already at rock bottom. I
was numb.

THE POWER OF DREAMS IS IN THE
LAW OF ATTRACTION

*"95% of achieving anything is knowing what you want and
being willing to pay the price to get it."*
- Unknown

The Law of Attraction states, "Situations where the universe seems unresponsive to people's wishes, despite them trying to attract results, occur due to the thoughts and energy created.

"If you are desperate to have something, you are in a state of need. Thus, you remain needy instead of becoming successful."

The universe receives your needy energy, and politely sends you more needy energy since it is programmed to deliver your primary focus."

"Good things happen when you are not experiencing the energy of need. Your life might still be enhanced greatly when you receive gifts from the universe, and in this sense, you require what you obtain. However, you are not urgently crying out for a result when it occurs."

If the Law of Attraction is real, maybe, just perhaps, up until this time I was too needy and didn't realize the need I had may have been blocking my success. That certainly seemed to be a plausible explanation to help me understand this most recent setback. My mother would often say, "Any old hat beats a derby." Don't ask me what that means or why I'm placing this random quote here; it just seems to fit.

Anyway, I was not prepared for what happened next. "Debra," Dr. Morrison said, "I'm going to be relocating to the Ann Arbor VA Medical Center. I'm taking the directorship of that hospital." I felt myself start to fidget with nervousness. He proceeded, "I'll have a satellite clinic in Toledo, Ohio that's going to need a clinic administrator."

I immediately thought, "That's nice! Why was he telling me this? Was it to rub in my face the fact that I'd never qualify for the position?" I'm thinking, "How cruel!" "Debra?" Dr. Morrison called out. For a moment, I was in a daze and couldn't hear him. "Debra?" Dr. Morrison called out to me again. Startled, I responded, "Yes Sir." He said, "I'd like you to consider moving to Toledo and running the outpatient clinic as my first in charge. You'd be the clinic administrator and the position is a GS-12." "Is that something that might be of interest to you?"

This time my right lung collapsed! This could not be happening. Just moments ago, I thought he crushed my dreams because I didn't have a college degree. How could he be offering me this job? My mind was racing. Does he have an ulterior motive? I don't think that for one minute if he did that it would have mattered, I immediately went into checklist mode:

- ✓ I'd have to leave San Diego and move to Toledo, Ohio. Check.
- ✓ I'd be the boss. Check.
- ✓ I would be promoted from a GS-10 to a GS-12. Check.

Sounded good to me, but there had to be a catch. While my checklist was playing in my head, Dr. Morrison continued and said, "Debra, if you accept this offer, you will need to enroll in the university and complete your education."

"Is this the catch," I thought? I was like, "Duh! I can do this." Add this to the checklist. How could I turn this opportunity down? Suddenly, things were shifting in my favor, and this wasn't the end of this incredible blessing. Dr. Morrison continued, "To sweeten the deal, we'll pay your relocation expenses and financially support you to help defray the costs of getting your college degree!"

If you have ever wondered whether God cares about your dreams and desires and healing your wounds, I'm here to tell you that He does! The Bible says in Jeremiah 17:14 (NLT), "God, pick up the pieces of my life. Put me back together again. I give you my praise." Without further thought or hesitation, I said, "I accept your generous offer."

"Breathless, I thought, "God must love chicks with scars!"

73

CHAPTER SIX:

YOU CHOOSE THE FACE OTHERS SEE

"I'm not interested in trying to work on people's perceptions. I am who I am, and if you don't take the time to learn about that, then your perception is going to be your problem."

-Jim Brown

"Every time you walk away from doing what makes you feel great something inside of you dies."

Making the decision to move across the country again was frankly an easy decision for me. There were no prohibiting factors. I was a 30-something, single, black female on my own, not attached to any man, owned no property and had no children a triple threat for real.

I'm sure there are plenty of women who would love to be able to move around the country and relocate for their career opportunities but can't because they have responsibilities that limit their mobility. Fortunately, for me, I was not that woman.

74

I was never the girl who had these constraints. I never wanted to be married and tied down in any way. It just wasn't my thing. I never saw myself as a wife or a mother and quite frankly, let me remind you, I evolved into hating marriage.

Don't get me wrong; although I hated marriage, I did have a healthy interest in the opposite sex. Sadly, something was always wrong. None of my relationships were healthy. I remember early at the start of my career in Chicago; I dated a co-worker who outranked me educationally and financially. I didn't completely understand what he saw in me, and naïvely, I thought our relationship was moving along nicely for a while until I learned he was embarrassed by the fact that I was his subordinate. He dropped me for a flight attendant. The very idea!

At this stage, what had I learned if anything, from the life I was creating? The only answer: nothing substantial! I decided no more looking back. I needed to focus and prepare myself to move to Toledo. The more I looked forward to the new prospects of a fresh start, the greater the spiritual attack became on my thought life.

Doubt reared its ugly head. How was I going to fit in? I knew nothing about the city of Toledo. I couldn't help but think, "Are there any black people in Toledo? Where will I live? Will I have any friends? Will people like me?" "Am I too old to be enrolling in college as a full-time student?"

I vividly remember my first day at work. I arrived around 7:00 am, to the VA Medical Center in Ann Arbor, Michigan. I was anxious. I reported early so I could walk around to scope things out. I needed to become familiar with my new surroundings.

Everyone I encountered was pleasant and engaging. They were accommodating and helpful. I remember thinking, "This is my new home." I thought, "I've made it! I'm living my dream." After completing the required HR paperwork, I quickly drove to the outpatient clinic in Toledo. When I walked in, I was somewhat overjoyed to see there were a handful of African Americans working at the clinic and they were all professionals.

Within the first week of adjusting to my new position, I enrolled at the University of Toledo, as a full-time student. I took a full course load. I went to school around the clock. I decided early that I would not take any breaks, not even during summer. I felt pressure to perform, and I could not disappoint Dr. Morrison. I had to get my degree as fast as I could.

With the stress of school and working full-time, the first few months I kept a full schedule. I did a "listening tour" so I could become acclimated, find my grounding and get to know the people.

I also had another agenda. I desperately wanted to make friends, because I needed to be accepted.

"When you experience rejection, it's a tough terrain to navigate. So naturally, you reach for the low-hanging fruit; that thing that makes you feel safe, accepted, secured and possibly, loved."

As time moved on, the ensuing months at the clinic became just plain weird. I wanted to get to know all the staff, but I could sense underlying tension and total disapproval. My initial thoughts were that it was due to me being a woman because I had moved passed that *black thing*.

When most people think of racism, they usually think of big, obvious examples, like the KKK or Nazis; but there are so many more complicated facets of this complex phenomenon. Racism can be far more subtle and insidious. Many people of color face casual, everyday racism more often than the more visible signs.

For example, if your colleagues invite others to dinner but not you, it is hard to know if it is because they've known each other for a longer time, or because they don't like you or because they are uncomfortable with people of your race.

Subtle discrimination mostly occurs in interactions with people who are close to you — like colleagues, your manager, your friends, and it's not very clear or explicit. Studies show that as the one experiencing the discrimination tries to determine what is going on, they are likely to examine their social role, including whether people around them accept them.

You might be wondering how there is any room for racism in the workplace, to begin with. After all, there are many laws put in place to combat and deal with this directly. However, racism in the workplace is often times not overt but is hidden under the guise of jokes or unfair treatment of certain individuals.

To my dismay, it became painfully obvious to me that a subtle form of racism was alive and well and living at the clinic. For example, I would be left out of department parties when all the other staff was invited to attend. I was never invited to hang out after work. I remember on two separate occasions, two women were getting married and neither of them invited me to their weddings. I would get asked purposely, "Are you going to so and so's wedding." I would answer, "No, I'm not invited." The person asking already knew I wasn't invited and wanted to humiliate me. I was convinced that all of this aggression was because I was black *and* the boss. Their behavior was unrelenting and cruel, it was hurtful, but I withstood.

"It was clear that no one wanted to align themselves with the new clinic administrator, *Ms. Blackenstein!* My self-esteem was eroding, and I found myself continuously appraising my abilities and my quality as a person."

I could not fathom how hate could be so overt yet subtle and so pervasive. These people didn't know me, and they were not interested in getting to know me. I spent hours trying to figure out why would anyone dislike someone for no apparent reason other than the color of his or her skin? The face I chose to show them was one of confidence, intelligence, and grit. I didn't flaunt my *blackness* nor did I try to hide it, I couldn't.

I would not let their behavior unsettle me. I did what I needed to do. I put on a thick layer of skin, sprinkled with a touch of arrogance. I gave them someone to dislike. I had to protect myself and assert my authority and remind these people *I WAS* the boss! I also began to notice that this malevolent attitude was apparent every time I attended a staff meeting or a special event in Ann Arbor.

I didn't imagine any of this conduct. These people were determined to bring so much pressure on me that I would buckle under the weight of it all and leave my *second chance*.

They underestimated this little black girl from the Southside. I let them know in no uncertain terms that I was there to stay and that I deserved to be there until I deserved to be removed. I did not deserve to be removed. I can't ever remember feeling so isolated.

I prayed that I would find and make a friend. I needed someone I could relate to. Someone I could talk to. Someone who would celebrate me, not just tolerate me. It wasn't long before God answered my prayers!

EVERY GIRL NEEDS A GFF (GIRLFRIEND FOREVER)

"Friendship isn't about who you've known the longest. It's about who walked into your life and said "I'm here for you" and proved it."
—Anonymous

81

One morning, an African-American female pharmaceutical rep came into the office to check in before her visit to host a lunch for the medical staff. I was stunned. Not because this woman was beautiful, but I was stunned because she was black!

Lisa peeked into my office. I think she was taken aback when she saw that a black woman was sitting in the *bosses' chair*. I invited her in, and we began to talk. She was somewhat shocked because in the time she spent working that territory, she never once saw a person of color occupy that office.

Lisa was witty and delightful, fun to be around and not to mention, drop dead gorgeous! I thought, "I have a new friend and ally, thank you, God!" I could feel myself navigating toward her because we had something in common: single African-American women putting it down in a white male dominated world.

Lisa became my GFF (girlfriend forever) and, we shared many adventures. We hung out all the time and spent all our available time together dining, shopping, and going to the movies. This was a perfect friendship.

As I was beginning to trust her, I found myself pouring out my heart to her about what was happening to me at the clinic. Lisa was empathetic and very encouraging. She reminded me that I was the one who was in control. I had the power.

She also told me something profound, which stuck with me, "People tend to fear what they don't understand." This empowered me. I was not going to be disrespected or pushed around. Lisa was good for my self-esteem and confidence. My sense of purpose and power was reignited.

"Isn't it amazing how one person can change your life? Not because there was something wrong or because you needed to; you've just subconsciously made a decision to better yourself because of them."

These are the people whom you look forward to speaking to every day. They can make your day with a simple "Hello." They brighten up your day just by being at your side.

They have the power to alter the way you think because you're able to see things from their perspective as well as your own. Just by spending time with someone, you tend to pick up their tendencies, their mannerisms, and their values without realizing it.

It's so nice to have that one person who takes the time to care about you and to give you good advice when you need it. For me that person was and still is today, Lisa.

I couldn't help but think about all the trials that I suffered were preparing me for something far greater. I chose a new face for people to see— my true face.

CHAPTER SEVEN:

IF LOVING YOU IS WRONG...

"Don't let the person who didn't love you, keep you from the person who will."

-Trent Shelton

Let's face it. We've all done it. We make mistakes. We make poor choices. Experts say we develop our taste in men at a young age— anywhere from childhood to adolescence. "Whether it's positive or negative, everyone has a relationship pattern based on what they learned about love when they were growing up," says Alon Gratch, Ph.D., author of *If Love Could Think.*

One evening after work, Lisa, my GFF and I decided to try a new spot that had just opened. They say when you meet someone; they have the ability to change your life forever. At the most unbelievable time and the most unlikely place, I met *My Favorite Mistake.* I had my GFF and miraculously, to our surprise, we discovered there were good looking professional black men living in Toledo! We were shocked, to say the least. The question was, "What rock had they been hiding under?"

A LIE BY ANY OTHER NAME…

"Lie: If the package is beautifully wrapped, its contents will be fabulous."
"Truth: The packaging doesn't tell you anything about what's inside."
–Dr. Robin Smith

What are toxic relationships? They are dead end ties. They are relationships that will never go anywhere. They are relationships with someone who isn't right for you or someone who is incapable of love or commitment. They are relationships which make you happy some of the time and which make you miserable the rest of the time.

"I'm talking about relationships where two people are either on different wavelengths or where they are not getting their needs met but stay in the relationship because there is

86

something about the other person which is compelling or habit-forming."

Because this person fulfills some extreme, basic need you have, you become addicted or dependent on that person and you unconsciously ignore the fact that this person cannot or will not fulfill some of your basic needs.

If you've been there, you understand the struggle. This might seem relatable to you if in most of your relationships you've somehow lost sight of who are and what things you stand for. Also, if you feel your confidence becomes more and more shot after each relationship, it's likely you're dating the wrong person. Now realize if you've dated one awful person, this doesn't necessarily mean you're addicted to bad relationships.

My Favorite Mistake and I hit it off instantly. He was everything I thought I might want in a man. He pretended to be marginally disinterested even though I could tell he was intrigued.

Initially, we both presented our best selves to each other. We talked incessantly. I was fascinated

87

with the idea of him. He was fascinated with the idea of me. It took some time but at some point, we wanted to share accessible parts of our lives, do some things together and form commonalities, which I thought would create a foundation for our future. I saw him as a man of influence. His charisma could light up the Grand Canyon at 15 minutes after midnight.

It didn't take long before I could tell that he needed to *fix* me, shape me into the model of a suitable woman. I wasn't offended and I didn't think I minded because he captivated me.

He cultivated me in more ways than one; he was instrumental in obtaining my appointment as an officer on the Board of Directors of a local homeless shelter, he introduced me to Hartmann Luggage, Coogi sweaters, Allen Edmond shoes, Hickey Freeman suits and Montblanc pens. He was a label whore. He made me into a label whore.

"I became addicted. *My favorite mistake* introduced me to many new ideas and

sensations I had never before experienced. I believed this was a sign of true love."

This man was larger than life and I wanted *this* life. When you are emotionally thirsty, you'll drink from the fountain of anyone you believe has *water*. Where did I end and where did he begin? Early in our relationship, I didn't know; I didn't even care.

I've never been a liar. I hate liars. I hate all forms of dishonesty. I believe the hallmark of an ethical human being is to be in the habit of openly telling the truth…even when it might make him/her look bad. I was so filled with self-doubt that I didn't trust anyone enough to tell the truth about myself openly, nor did I feel worthy of having a man of his stature.

I frantically needed him to not only like me but to fall head over heels in love with me completely. I had to do something radical to impress him. I had to do something drastic. I wasn't going to be left behind for another flight attendant. I was so afraid he wouldn't like the *real* me.

If I had only believed that what you truly are is so much greater than what you have or pretend to be, I could have saved myself from myself.

I know this is true, but maybe more often for some, and maybe always for others, we have been beaten down by life, and our inner being diminishes. This is when Satan does his greatest work.

Satan reminds us when our efforts are not enough. We then begin to collect our failures like scrapbook mementos, a mental book we pull out to remind us to act in a way that is limited because that is who we really are. "Didn't we fail at this or that? Weren't our efforts second rate and unacknowledged? Don't we have to honestly say that our best talents are but a wisp of the wind?" We strategically remind ourselves. "Don't we have plenty of evidence for all the above? (Evidence gladly supplied by the enemy himself.) You are not much," says Satan to us. "You have never been much." With the veil dropped over our minds, in our amnesiac state, we believe him.

This is why it was so easy for me, a woman, who loved God and hated lying, to not only fabricate but also live a lie. I heard those voices in my head taunting me. I let the enemy lure me and steal my identity in Christ. I fell for his lies and created a character that did not exist. This character was sophisticated, well-traveled and working on her master's degree.

"Debra, the little black girl from the southside of Chicago, disappeared. I completely erased myself. I don't know who this new woman was; I never gave her a name. I only knew the disguise was important because I had believed that it's what you see in the first moment of attraction that will determine if you will be together."

This man was alluring. He was educated, dapper, belonged to the same fraternity as my father, and he was a high-powered executive. In my twisted thinking, there was no way I could ruin my chance at a relationship with the *perfect package*. How in the world did he wind up in Toledo anyway?

91

My Favorite Mistake was arrogant and smug because he could be. He taught me how to be arrogant and smug; traits that I thought would serve me well in my position at work. I occupied my thoughts during the day with fantasies about how we could become the ultimate power couple and dominate Ohio. He was incredibly shallow, but in the back of my mind, that didn't matter.

I could tell he was becoming intrigued with the person I led him to believe I was. I found myself sinking deeper and deeper into a relationship that was built on lies; not to mention with a man I later discovered didn't deserve the *real* me.

"Shortly into our relationship, *my favorite mistake* told me my initial appeal to him was the fact that I was single, didn't have any children, and I had good hair! Yes, he said it, and yes, I believed it to be a compliment."

Despite his superficiality, I figured I would never do better than him, so I stayed in hot pursuit of this relationship. The longer I played along, the more I began to learn about his character. His true colors were bursting off his canvas. I finally forced myself to realize that he was window dressing; there was much in the window, but nothing in the room.

I had to be crazy to think our relationship would be anything more than unstable. We had been seeing each other for months when I accidentally on purpose learned that he was involved with another woman at his workplace. When I refer to accidentally on purpose, I'm talking about the fact that my insecurities forced me to search through his phone, his computer, and his house. I interrogated his children. That's when I found *her, the other woman*! I also discovered that they had been in a relationship for quite some time, longer than two years and exploring the possibility of marriage!

WTH! Oh, no he didn't! Yes, boo, he did! This was ludicrous. How could he do this to me? I must be stone cold crazy. The irony in all of this was why would I expect fidelity and honesty from him when I couldn't even tell him the truth about myself?

"In a rush of anger and stupidity — side note, the angrier you become, the stupider you get because the blood flow leaves your brain and travels to your extremities which triggers your fight or flight response."

There was no way that I was remotely about to let my labor be in vain. I was not about to lose out to another woman, especially after I worked so hard to get this man.

The blood-deprived part of my brain convinced me that I would fight for him, rather than allow him to fight for me. The thought of him fighting for me didn't matter much because no man had ever fought for me before. I actually believed this was *love*.

EYES WIDE OPEN

"Everything happens for a reason. But sometimes the reason is that you're stupid and you make bad decisions."
-Anonymous

White lies and half-truths can cause havoc and shrink a relationship into nothing faster than a cold dunk into ice water. When I confronted him about his deceit, he smugly declared, "What made you think I was tied to any one woman?"

What? My heart was crushed! The warning signs were there, and I ignored them all.

"It hurts when you realize that you aren't as important to someone as you thought you were. Through heartbreak, you come to see yourself as rejected, dejected, failed and damaged."

I was humiliated, embarrassed and depressed. I retreated. I lied in my bed for a while, quite convinced the pain and unhappiness of wanting someone who didn't want me, was going to be my undoing. I wallowed in the misery of it all. Heartbreak squeezes you as though you were an orange, crushes you as though it were a tractor, and cuts sharply as a razor blade.

The path of spiritual healing is a powerful one, and in few places, is healing so sorely needed as in the realm of our hearts. Broken hearts can lead to awakened souls. Miraculously, something touched my spirit.

My broken heart connected me to the fact I had a power leak, and it had to be plugged. There was a breach in my vertical relationship with God; I had to restore it. My relationship with God was not broken because of anything God had done, but because of what I had done.

I turned away from God's standards and made my own path; this path could not be sustained.

"What had I learned from living a life of lies and half-truths? I had no other choice than to tell myself the truth about the liar in my life...especially since that liar was me!"

I had to look at myself and ask if I liked what I saw on the inside and out. The answer was **NO**! I hated who I had become. I hated the fact that my spirit was so broken that I stooped to deceit and manipulation.

Something had to change, and at that moment, I determined that what needed to change was me. I was no longer going to shut myself away from the world. I was no longer going to ignore all the good things that were out there with my name stamped on them.

I purposed to own my true self. From now on, I would live my life with my eyes wide open, a life of appreciation, a life of simplicity, a life of happiness, and life with peace of mind.

In the following months, I learned more about myself than I had in my entire lifetime, and in applying those lessons to my everyday life, I became truly happy and deeply appreciative of the world around me.

I also discovered the strength of the power within me. I realized no one would ever love me as much as I can love myself. No one is worth sacrificing my values over. I decided I was going to change and grow a little each day. This was a painful but necessary lesson, and I learned it.

I realized nothing should be more important than self-respect and knowing your true worth. I needed to choose myself, not in a selfish manner but in a way, that allowed me to make healthy decisions that would produce healthy outcomes. I made a commitment to love and trust myself above all others.

Today, I am a firm believer that...

"you should never invest yourself in a relationship with someone who does not value you. You should never have to convince someone to love you. And you must never, never, ever lose your relationship and identity in Christ."

CAN IT GET ANY WORSE?

"What I feared has come upon me; what I dreaded has happened to me."
— Job 3:25

The only common denominator in every one of my failed relationships was me. They say hindsight is 20/20; that's because usually at the end of a broken relationship you can see all the evidence from along the way that this one isn't going to last. I finally recognized *My Favorite Mistake's* behavior for what it was. This was hard for me, especially after I put so much time and energy into making it work. I let him go, and I could honestly say I tried. Could my life get any worse?

It's 1993. Dr. Morrison called me to tell me he was taking an assignment in Montana. I immediately thought, "There's no way I'm moving to Montana." It was funny I thought this because ironically, he didn't offer to take me with him. His transfer came quickly and just like that, *poof*, he was gone. My mentor, protector, and confidant was gone.

I was left to fend for myself. Deep in the recesses of my mind, when I agreed to accept this position, I feared this would happen. I would be left alone. My fear was now my reality. How in the world was I going survive in this hostile environment without my mentor? Who would protect me? I certainly didn't have a man to protect me. I had to protect myself. To make matters worse, my relationship with *My Favorite Mistake* was irrevocably broken.

CLEAR AND PRESENT DANGER

"If only closed minds came with closed mouths."
– Anonymous

Dr. Jones, the Chief of Staff, who was appointed acting director, hated me. Period. It didn't take him long to begin his retaliation campaign to *blackball* me, no pun intended. He did everything he could to ramp up pressure for me to quit. He did not want me on staff. He did not understand nor did he appreciate the relationship I enjoyed with Dr. Morrison.

His staff was instructed to make my work life a living hell. Every action I took was scrutinized. I couldn't do anything right. I walked on eggshells while looking over my shoulders. I couldn't even trust my secretary because I felt she had been turned against me too. They worked overtime to catch me doing something that could be used against me.

100

The lowest point of this attack happened when I was summoned to the medical center for a meeting with the acting director. In that meeting, Dr. Jones prefaced our conversation by saying,

"Debra, the first time I ever saw a black person, I was 17 years old." He continued, "I was 20 years old before I ever saw a woman in a role of authority." He concluded with, "I don't know what to do with you, a black female in a position of power."

Wow! I was in suspended disbelief. How ignorant can this person be? Did Dr. Jones just say these incredibly racist and sexist things to me out loud? How could he, in good conscious, fix his mouth to say these vile things to my face? Was this man raised by a pack of wolves? Did he live in a cave cut off from the world, cut off from the diversity that is America?

The hatred and contempt he felt towards me were palpable. Was I some freakish anomaly that would never fit into his white man's view of an *'ideal'*

101

world? This was my first encounter with overt racism. It's easier to shrug off overt discrimination because you can attribute it to irrational behavior on the part of the other person. You don't have to examine yourself or the situation too closely. Overt discrimination — such as Dr. Jones' racist remarks, is a clear form of prejudice. No wonder the staff at the clinic felt empowered to discriminate against me. They were only taking on the character of their leadership.

Being an African-American woman in a position of authority in a white male dominated world, always come with challenges and stereotyping.

"If you are too authoritarian, you're an angry black woman. If you *shuck and jive*, you're not taken seriously. You become a caricature; a joke; I was determined to be neither."

Workplace discrimination is hideous. I felt anxious, angry, confused, and violated. In this state of mind, it was difficult for me to formulate a course of action to resolve the problem. However, there was no way I was going to let this stand. I had to fight back. I filed an EEO complaint to no avail. Since he was the boss, the people in charge of EEO complaints only went through the motions. They were never going to take my case seriously, and no one would rule in my favor.

I was tired of being harassed; this was taking its toll on me. However, I endured. I was not going to be intimidated and forced out of a job that I deserved. I worked hard all my life for this opportunity, and the *gates of hell would not prevail against me*. I would only make a move on my terms.

I finally decided that the time had come for me to find a safer environment where I could thrive personally and professionally. The threat of danger had to be removed. It was time for major changes in every area of my life.

CHAPTER EIGHT:

LOVE THE PROCESS... IT WILL GET YOU THE RESULTS.

"There is no substitute under the heavens for productive labor. It is the process upon which dreams become realities. It is the process by which idle visions become dynamic achievements."

-Gordon B. Hinckley

My last year in Toledo was traumatic, both personally and professionally. It was time for me to set a new course, a new beginning. It was time for me to find a new home. I began to apply for positions across the country. I didn't care where I landed; I just needed to land somewhere else, safely. I must have applied for over seventy-five jobs. Every application I submitted was returned with the infamous response, "Considered but Not Selected." I believed that after over seventy-five 'Not Selected' there had to be a yes coming for me soon. I knew I was being undermined, but I reminded myself that I hadn't worked this hard to overcome so much that I would give up now. I paid my dues. I had my battle scars. I won.

THE STRUGGLE IS REAL

"The struggle is real but so are the blessings."
–Anonymous

"When God tests you, or bad stuff happens, we need to see it as a time to learn and to trust him by changing what is wrong in our lives while putting his promises in our hearts."

And when it is over we can look back and see that our trials have been necessary. We are better; He is glorified!

Struggle has its reward. What I couldn't understand was, "Why now, do I have to struggle?" What is God trying to teach me? Is He trying to sharpen me? What's His plan? How does any of this fit into my dreams?

I was in a place in my life that I thought to struggle was for other people; certainly, not for me. The Holy Spirit revealed the truth that struggles:

- Tests our identity as Christians. When we deal with tribulation, as we should, it authenticates our true identity as believers.

- Tests our faith. "These [trials] have come so that your faith of greater worth than gold, which perishes even though refined by fire may be proved genuine and may result in praise, glory and honor when Jesus Christ is revealed" 1 Peter 1:7 (NKJ).

- Tests our sense of purpose. Conflict tests our obedience. "The reason I wrote you was to see if you would stand the test and be obedient in everything" 2 Corinthians 2:9 (NIV).

- Tests to teach us to rely on God. "We do not want you to be uninformed, brothers, about the hardships we suffered in the province of Asia. We were under great pressure, far beyond our ability to endure, so that we despaired even of life. Indeed, in our hearts we felt the sentence of death. But this happened that we might not rely on ourselves but on God, who raises the dead. He has delivered us from such a deadly peril, and he will deliver us. On him we have set our hope that he will continue to deliver us, as you help us by your prayers. Then many will give thanks on our behalf for the gracious favor granted us in answer to the prayers of many" 2 Corinthians 1:8-11(NIV).

- Tests us so that it will go well with us. "He gave you manna to eat in the desert, something your fathers had never known, to humble and to test you so that in the end it might go well with you" Deuteronomy 8:16 (NIV).

With everything that I just suffered, I knew that there was a force working against me. This force was not for my good, but for my destruction. I cried out, "God, I need you!"

God answered. January 12, 1994, I got my *yes*! I was notified that I had been selected for the position of Implementation Manager with the Decision Support System. If I accepted the position, I would need to report for my new duties by March 31, 1994. In disbelief, I simply thought, "But God!"

If we stay the course and faint not, God is able to do exceedingly above and beyond anything we could ever imagine. It's funny that even though I was operating outside of the Will of God, He never lost sight of this little black girl.

"We need to see life as a series of problem-solving and learning opportunities because the problems we face will either overwhelm and overpower us, or grow and develop us. The paths of joy is determined by how we respond to our struggles, tests and trials."

Unfortunately, most people including Christians will fail to see God's hand in their life. Choosing instead to focus on their problem and allowing it to take over their lives.

God wants to use our problems for good, to make us better and stronger for our personal development and in turn for us to be able to help others. If you love the process, it will get you the results.

DID HISTORY JUST REPEAT ITSELF?

"There are only patterns, patterns on top of patterns, patterns that affect other patterns. Patterns hidden by patterns. Patterns within patterns. If you watch close, history does nothing but repeat itself."
-Chuck Palahniuk

My new assignment was in Milwaukee, Wisconsin. I called my biggest cheerleader, my father. I was exuberant and unable to contain my joy. I called him and said, "Daddy, I'm going to be working in Milwaukee, but I don't want to live there. I'd rather commute from Chicago on a weekly basis until I decide where I want to relocate."

Understand, that this commute wouldn't bother me because the government paid my travel expenses. I asked, "Can I move back home until I get my permanent assignment?" Enthusiastically, dad said,

"Of course, little deb, come home." This was music to my ears. I moved back to the comfort of my youth."

As time progressed, I was emotionally strong enough that I periodically kept in touch with *My Favorite Mistake*. I wasn't surprised when he called to tell me about a new job opportunity he was offered. Ironically, it was in Milwaukee. After our history of course, I was cynical. *Yeah, right. New opportunity my foot!* I knew that this was more than just a coincidence. He was aware that I was working in Milwaukee. I then remembered that right before I left Toledo, he vowed that we would eventually be together and that he would not give up. At this stage in my life, none of this mattered because there was no way I would allow myself to get sucked back in. I had a new outlook. I had a renewed mind. I was no longer insane.

The *bloodline in the sand* was real. I made myself clear that we would *never* get back together.

I'm not going to lie, what's the point? His news caused me to reflect back to when we were together. I thought about how I surrendered who I was and how I sacrificed myself on the altar of his acceptance. I remembered being unrecognizable. I wasn't going to get trapped again.

Who was I kidding? The thought of resurrecting our relationship was frightening yet intriguing. Deep down, where it counts, I never stopped loving this man. Why was being with someone who never actually loved me, honored nor valued me, an option?

I had experience that proved that what we shared was **not** love. I also knew repeating the past wouldn't create a new future; repeating the past would only add more harm and hurt. "Wake up girl," the still small voice within me shouted. "You've been given a second chance at your dreams!"

"We get two chances to decide; your first decision can be a mistake; the second decision is not a mistake, it's a choice."

I vowed that I would not welcome this distraction back into my life. I had to remember that I was working at a new level. I had to bring my *A-game*; I had no time for trouble. This was not the time to shift my focus. I couldn't allow any disruptions to my plan. This self-talk grounded me.

Guess what happened next?

Why do we always go back to previous relationships that fell apart? Why do we go back to people that have hurt us? Why do we go back when it clearly didn't work? We do this because we're creatures of habit. How easy is it to go back to someone with the hope that they'll finally change this time? We often think, "I'm more mature now," or "It'll be different this time." More often, than not, we lie to ourselves. It's not to say some people won't change or that trying again is a waste of time; not at all.

However, sometimes certain people don't work well together. No matter how much you care about that person, or how much you love him or her, it was never meant to be. Yeah, that hurts. Yeah, that realization sucks, but honestly, that's life.

As *My Favorite Mistake* settled into his new position in Milwaukee, I looked forward to seeing him when I was in town. He convinced me, and I believed, that this time around we had a chance for a healthy relationship. Why would two seemingly intelligent people fall back into the same trap? Probably because old habits die hard and familiar fruit tastes good.

It didn't take long for us to return to our default, lying. In a frantic effort to self-preserve, I went back to fear-based behaviors. I became obsessed to the extent I was more controlling and jealous than I had ever been before. I needed to know everything about what he was doing, where he was going, and who he spoke with on the phone. I knew I couldn't trust him and I desperately wanted him to treat me right. Why wasn't I good enough?

When I think about all of this craziness, I believe that we were codependent. I didn't understand it then, but I certainly understand it now.

"The nature of codependence is continually seeking what is familiar, but what is not necessarily good."

Who could I blame but myself for being so naïve? I thought our breakup the first time *fixed* him. This time around, all I saw was the person I hoped he'd become. The question now was, where was the woman *I* had become?

I finally faced myself. I knew if I didn't stop the madness, I would be forever trapped in a life that was non-conducive to my spiritual and emotional growth. I came to terms with the fact that if I wanted to achieve my dreams and walk in my passion, I had to let him go.

The sobering reality was I needed to focus on the next part of the process that would get me the results I desired. This is precisely the path I needed to choose to achieve the goals I wanted.

"To leave from where you are, you must decide where you would rather be, and then make the changes necessary to get there."

The process, the doing, is in the now! A desired future outcome is nothing more than a picture, in the now. The future is an illusion rooted in faith.

I learned to see my future for what it was: a state of being I create in the now. I could not escape this moment. I had to choose to appreciate what was happening now. Eventually, if you love the process, it will get you the results. Trust me, I know!

A CHANGE IS GOING TO COME

"Change is hard at first, messy in the middle, and gorgeous at the end."
-Robin Sharma

"Without change, nothing changes."

The changes needed in your life may sometimes call for a new start. I was not going to get stuck in a quagmire of quicksand; chained to my past, slowly asphyxiating from every hurt, disappointment, lie, and betrayal. I was no longer a prisoner. I realized love and obsessions are not the same. Surrendering the need to control other people helps you to connect with yourself.

I had to get back to living **my** dreams — the dreams that wouldn't hurt or disappoint me. If I was ever going to realize my passions and my dreams, I had to have a Deuteronomy 30:19 experience. I had to choose life.

There comes a time you must learn if you're on a road that leads nowhere, and then you must travel a different path. If you don't like *how the table is set*, turn the table over! I took that advice and turned over the table. I ended things permanently with *My Favorite Mistake*.

Don't ever underestimate God's power. By choosing life, God handily orchestrated another opportunity that would free me from a labyrinth of sorrow and set me on a new trajectory to freedom.

CHAPTER NINE:

IT'S ALL ABOUT ME!

"Self-care is not self-indulgence. Self-care is self-respect."

-Anonymous

Confidence and performance are closely linked.

"Confidence is a game of momentum."

Being able to project confidence enables people to believe in you, setting you up for success, and that success brings even more confidence. Your level of confidence not only determines the expectations people have for you, but it also establishes the expectations you have for yourself. Those expectations then set the limit on your performance. And the way you perform affects the confidence you have in your abilities.

If there is a chance, then there is a possibility— a way to achieve whatever it is you wish or want to achieve. Understanding that these possibilities, no matter how unlikely, are available and can develop

117

into existence, may help you make it out of the deepest, darkest holes.

When bouncing from disappointment to disappointment, it's hard not to become cynical. But there's cynical, and there's being realistic. I learned to tell the difference between the two. It helped me to ask myself whether my attitude helped or hindered me.

All of my life, I wanted to be successful. Failure was not an option. The pressure to perform was not artificial; it was very real. In that pressure cooker, I came to realize that you do not come across success just by hoping for it. To achieve true success, you need the strength of mind and body to struggle and work hard to reach your fullest potential. You need the right attitude, self-discipline and the ability to put your goals before your own needs if you are driven towards achieving success. There is, after all, no substitute for hard work, and as Henry Ford says, "The harder you work, the luckier you get" – the more successful you get!

My first year working in Milwaukee proved to be a blessing in so many ways once I looked past the

118

darkness. The challenges I faced were no different from any other person who had a strong desire for a new start. I made new friends, and I worked hard to improve my self-confidence, my self-worth and my value. I proved to myself that I had what it took to succeed.

"The truth is, you can become someone worthy of respect, and someone who can pursue what you want despite the naysaying of others. You can do this by taking control of your life, and taking control of your self-confidence."

By taking concrete actions that improve your competence and your self-image, you can increase that confidence, without the help of anyone else.

I tested the results of my renewed self-confidence. I was ready. I was prepared. I took a risk and applied for and was selected for a GS-14 upper management position. I had no idea that this position would be the gateway toward the dreams that God had established for me.

MY NEW HOPE

"May your choices reflect your hopes, not your fears."
– Nelson Mandela

"I was in Washington, DC when *it* happened."

At the first staff meeting for the team of newly hired managers, one of the agenda items was to address how we were going to approach and implement the new healthcare initiative mandate for all VA medical centers across the United States.

We decided the most optimal approach would be to cluster VA facilities geographically. It's important to note here that I had no previous or pre-conceived notions about what our meeting would entail. Also, at this meeting, I never knew ahead of time that I would be making a life altering decision in a split second.

When was the last time you did something spontaneous? Something that that didn't fit into

120

your five-year plan, that took you outside of your comfort zone…just because.

I'm not a Richard Branson fan per se. If you're not familiar with Richard, he's the founder of Virgin, a company that does just about everything. He's also a daredevil and sets off on a moment's notice to hot air balloon across the Atlantic or base jump from the top of a skyscraper. His autobiography, "Losing My Virginity," explores how he has chosen to live his life. He often picks the unusual path for difficult decisions, not because it contributes most to the bottom line, but because in his gut it just feels right. Sometimes, he sets off on a crazy adventure just for the story.

In fact, he's run his life and his business with the mantra "screw it, let's do it." When something feels right, he commits to it and then figures out how to make it work after.

I had a Richard Branson moment during our meeting. Without reluctance, second thought, hesitation or a bathroom break, I blurted out loudly that I would take managerial responsibility for all the VA medical centers on the West coast. My only caveat was that I would be allowed to move to Phoenix, Arizona. After I had said it, I thought, "That was a random request, especially since I had never been to Phoenix."

My boss quickly took me up on my Branson moment and said, "Make it happen." Now,

"I was officially locked in with a date for my destiny. Looking back on this day, I had no idea why I said what I said, but God did."

I was excited about my move to Phoenix. This was going to be my permanent change of duty station. A new home, a *permanent* home. The anticipation of this fresh start was scary and exhilarating, which produced a converging of two entirely different emotions that rendered me speechless.

The possibilities were endless; especially since I was determined, I was going to get it right finally. I was no longer fascinated with foolishness. This was my time to re-create the life I wanted to live.

BLOOM WHERE YOU ARE PLANTED!

"For a seed to achieve its greatest expression, it must come completely undone. The shell cracks, its insides come out and everything changes. To someone who doesn't understand growth, it would look like complete destruction."
–Cynthia Occelli

November 12, 1995, the day I arrived in Phoenix, I checked into a hotel in Mesa and received a telephone call from my manager, Melissa. She said stoically, "Debra, what is the fax number to your hotel? I need to send you your pink slip." I said, "Melissa, what on earth are you talking about?" She then responded, "The Government has just been shut down, and we no longer have the authority to operate!" "WHAT!" I exclaimed. This was my first experience with something so absurd; I could only ask, "How in the world do you shut down an apparatus like the Federal Government?" This is crazy.

Fear quickly settled in because I just moved across the country at the Government's expense.

123

What was going to happen to me? Crippled by fear, I proceeded to ask myself, "Who was going to pay for my relocation expenses and my living allowance until I could find a place to live?"

I asked Melissa all these questions, and she didn't have any other answer for me except, "Until further notice, you are on your own." "Keep watching the news for updates." Unbelievable, I thought. This could not be happening, but in fact, it was happening in full force.

I called my father trembling. I had no idea what I was going to do.

"I cringed at the thought that my father would use this as an opportunity to give me the classic "I told you so" lecture. I had to admit that my father was right about everything he ever said to me,"

especially about my irresponsible spending habits; I spent all the money I earned on clothes and shoes. I didn't have any significant savings from which I could withdraw.

124

All I could hear playing in my head was my father's admonition, "Little Deb, instead of putting all of your money on your back, you should try and put some in the bank." You have no idea how bad I wished I had heeded his advice.

Surprisingly, my father was so proud of me that he didn't say, "I told you so." On the contrary, he was content to help me any way he could. For the umpteenth time, my father reassured me. He told me, "Lil' Deb, don't worry about a thing." My dad immediately wired me $3k to get me through the next two weeks. I was so grateful!

During this time, the first government shutdown lasted two weeks. Subsequently, the second government shutdown lasted a week. In the aftermath of the shutdowns, my employer, *the Federal Government*, released my back pay and paid my relocation expenses. I was relieved and honored to repay my father's *investment* in me with interest. Daddy was *tickled pink*! I knew it was time for me to finally grow up and bloom where I'm planted.

THE RESPONDENT

"A woman's heart must be so hidden in God that a man has to seek Him to find her.
– *Maya Angelou*

No matter how old you are and what stage of life you're at, uprooting your entire world and relocating to a new city can be a nerve-wracking experience. Between finding new neighborhood favorites, maintaining sociability, and overcoming anxiety, the whole move can leave you feeling mentally, emotionally, and physically exhausted.

After the dust had settled after the government shutdown, I found a beautiful townhouse to rent, and I was excited to finally have my household belongings delivered to my new address so I could make this place my home. I could barely wait to fill my home with my personality. I was so busy that the thought of meeting a man never crossed my mind. In fact, I was completely resolute with my status: single, black, female!

When I use the words "men" and "rebound" in the same sentence, male minds might quickly

126

conjure up thoughts of their favorite NBA teams. Women, however, understand that I am addressing the phenomenon of rushing into a new relationship after the dissolution of an old one.

"In a rebound relationship, it's common that the *rebound* is viewed as perfect – the person that we always wished we'd found first, and were so lucky to find this time. It's euphoric."

This response has a lot to do with our attachment needs seeking a state of stability to resolve the emotional crisis we have experienced after the last breakup. Metaphorically, we end up plugging all of our emotional strings deeply into the *rebounder* all at once, to emotionally stabilize ourselves.

I hadn't quite finished decorating and settling into my new life when I met *The Respondent*. We first met at a local hole in the wall restaurant where a lot of their patrons were well connected, highly respected, professional African-Americans.

127

This place was well known for their First Friday fish fry. I will admit this *joint* had the best-fried catfish I'd ever eaten.

The Respondent, like *My Favorite Mistake*, was attractive, tall, educated, a frat brother, and a professional. One trait I noticed and ignored between these two men was that neither of them ever professed their faith openly, and neither of them attended church; this should have been a HUGE red flag, but I overlooked it. Neither of them even discussed having a relationship with God.

"A word of caution to all of the single women reading my story, a man who truly cares about you will lead you to Christ, not to his bed!"

I remember my first date with *The Respondent*. He was so handsome, a 6'3" drink of mocha latte! He was such a gentleman and a breath of fresh air. Completely transparent. I was blown away by his honesty. He was divorced, and he shared with me that after his divorce, he delved into some reckless behaviors. Who was I to judge? I could relate.

He confided in me that one of his dalliances resulted in a one-night stand, which changed his life completely and produced the birth of his son. I couldn't help but think, "Why is he telling me all of this?" He could have lied. I was very familiar with lies. I was conditioned and prepared to expect lies. Instead, he chose truth. My hope was renewed that good men were not extinct. He was a rare breed.

We were instantly attracted to each other and very quickly started dating exclusively. It didn't take me long to fall for the man I thought he was. I believed he felt the same way. Welcome to Groundhog Day!

I took a risk with my heart, *again*. I was still unsure about relationships and marriage at this point because of my past, but there was something about him that made me reconsider having a long term, fully committed relationship. We connected and bonded in every way possible. I couldn't help but think that this time, I finally got it right.

He was the one my heart craved.

"He was the course correction for *my favorite mistake*. He was the perfect *rebounder*."

Outside of work, we spent ALL of our time together. Before I knew it, I gave him a key to my *castle*, which he happily accepted. He moved in without *officially* moving in. This went against every one of my core values.

My new job required extensive travel. *The Respondent* would drop me off and pick me up from the airport. He stayed at my townhouse while I was away. I continued to rationalize my behavior even though it violated every inch of my belief system. As far as I was concerned, this was an acceptable compromise because he was everything *My Favorite Mistake* wasn't and this enamored me. He was intentional about romance. He found my *sweet spot* and made sure he hit it every time. I couldn't help but think, *"Wow, this man has raised the bar!"*

He planned excursions for us, and we spent every waking day and all holidays together. I introduced him to my mom and my aunt; he was the *one*! We had plenty of talks about our future, which included marriage. I was open to the idea. I was serious; you might even say delirious.

Now, I'm 37 and happier than I had been in a long time; I've fallen in love with the perfect man. What else could happen? Oh yeah, I almost forgot, I'm also pregnant, again.

DOES THAT MAKE ME CRAZY?

"If you're not doing some things that are crazy, then you're doing the wrong things."
-Larry Page

"What woman in her right mind would take everything she worked so hard to accomplish and throw it all away?"

It's not just that I wasn't trying; I made every effort not to get pregnant. The news that I was indeed pregnant was shocking, to say the least. I was emotionally and spiritually shaken to my core. The fear I felt was incapacitating.

1 John 4:18 says, "There is no fear in love, but perfect love casts out all fear. For fear has to do with punishment, and whoever fears has not been perfected in love." (NIV) I was filled with fear, and I didn't feel God's perfect love. All I felt was torment.

My Lord, what have I done? The last thing I wanted or needed at this stage in my life was to be pregnant. How was I going to tell *The Respondent*? Would he be happy? How was I ever going to be able to explain this to my boss? I was just promoted. What impact would this have on my career? Would I still be able to travel?

Reality quickly set in. I saw myself as a stereotype: black female, old, unmarried and pregnant. Was this going to be my fate? I wanted my career more than anything. If I had to choose, hands down, career would win every time. I honestly didn't see myself as being mother *material*; this was not in the cards for me. I was so self-absorbed I couldn't make time for motherhood.

132

So, before you ask, yes, I considered an abortion (without my father's influence); so much so that I made the appointment. I was in full-blown unexpected crisis mode. I could make this problem go away and get back to my life. *The Respondent* never had to know.

"I clearly knew my vertical relationship with God was fractured."

The fact that I was thinking about an abortion was proof. I left my faith walk, and compromised my witness, but thank God; He made me a promise that He would never leave me nor forsake me.

DIVINE APPOINTMENT

"Be aware of divine appointments in your life. They can take you places you never imagined you would go."
–Pam Russell

Have you ever had a divine appointment? I have. Let me tell you what these miraculous interventions are: divine appointments are meetings with others that have been specifically and unmistakably ordered by God. Yet,

"I sometimes wondered how many of these supernaturally scheduled meetings I've missed, because I didn't have *my spiritual radar* turned on."

The Scriptures say, "The steps of a righteous man are ordered by the Lord." After decades of walking (off and on, but mostly on) with God, I can tell you that seeing God set up this appointment saved me from a spiritual death.

I've had many people play important roles in my life. Many of these people blessed me in so many ways. I look back now and realize it could have only been GOD who arranged these divine appointments.

I telephoned my friend, Tony, who I've known for over 20 years. I needed an objective ear; someone I had trust in and who would help me with my crisis. I was looking for someone to *sign off*

134

on my insanity; this way, I would feel justified about the choice I was about to make. My thinking was if someone I trusted agreed with me, then I would know I was making the right decision.

Tony listened to me rail on for over an hour about my circumstances and how I could not become a mother at this point in my life. Every word out of my mouth was about me, me, and me! It was all about me.

After patiently listening to me go on and on, Tony got my attention when he interrupted me and just stated, "Deb, you could be carrying the next prophet, the next president, or the person with a cure for cancer! Why would you interfere with their destiny?"

This revelation hit me like a casino being blown up on the Las Vegas strip! Tony gave me something compelling to think about. His counsel was godly, righteous and sobering. The Bible says in Proverbs 11:14, "Without good direction, people lose their way; the more wise counsel you follow, the better your chances." (The Message (MSG)). I tell you, if you have any trouble in your life, the best thing you can do is trust God.

My circumstance caused me to think about the story in the Bible of Shadrach, Meshach and Abednego, which gives an excellent example of how God's favor can deliver anyone from disaster. King Nebuchadnezzar gave a command for all the people to bow down and worship a gold image of him.

After Shadrach, Meshach and Abednego refused, they were bound and thrown into a fire. But God was in the furnace with them. And while they were in the worst moment of their life, they were loosed from those bondages. They went in bound but came out free. When they came out, they weren't scorched nor did they smell like smoke!

No matter where you are right now or what you've been through, if you'll let God in, He'll bring complete restoration to your life. God will schedule a divine appointment with you. I know because He scheduled an appointment for me.

"Early on in my life, I had a broken spirit. I didn't know how to think right. I thought

wrong about everything. God stepped into my life, and I came out on the other side, and I didn't smell like smoke either."

I felt a sense of peace come over me that I had never experienced before. I canceled my appointment. The shame I felt was overwhelming. Yet, I was grateful.

I had to tell *The Respondent* I was pregnant and confess what I had almost done. I naturally assumed we would get married and try to live life the right way before God. Especially since we had talked about our desire to have a future and, the fact that we were *shacking up*, this would be a natural progression for our relationship.

After telling him the news, I was relieved and encouraged. I gleefully asked him what he wanted to do about our relationship after I told him I was pregnant. To my astonishment, *The Respondent* laughed in my face and mockingly told me I couldn't make him marry me.

He continued harshly, "The days of the 'shotgun wedding' are over!" At that moment, my soul was

137

crushed, again. How in the world could this be happening to me a second time? My default impulses kicked in, the only way to protect my hurt would be by manipulation and control. I threatened him with everything I could think of to persuade him to marry me. I ranted that I would not give his child his name nor would I allow him to have a relationship with the baby.

When that didn't work, I told him he could move in with me permanently. I tried to convince him this was the *right* thing to do. He didn't agree, but he certainly leaped at the opportunity to move out of his mother's attic and move into my house. I was desperate and emotionally hungry. This was completely unimaginable.

FIGHTING FOR LIFE!

"Above all, children need our unconditional love, whether they succeed or make mistakes; when life is easy and when life is tough."

-President Barack Obama

My pregnancy was difficult, to say the least. My doctors labeled it a *geriatric pregnancy* because I was over 35. Due to my medical history, my pregnancy was also categorized as 'high risk.' I almost miscarried twice. To prevent a blood clot from forming, I had to administer Heparin injections twice daily into my abdomen throughout my pregnancy, and six weeks post-delivery.

I needed to have two amniocenteses. The first was to determine if there were any genetic defects with the baby, and the second was to determine if my baby's lungs were developed enough to allow her to breathe on her own at the time of premature delivery.

My doctors, who were neonatologists (physicians who specialize in complex, high-risk pregnancies), planned delivery by Caesarean section five weeks before full term. I was in constant pain. I thought, "Maybe this was God's way of punishing me for considering terminating my pregnancy." I had no right to complain.

Jordyn Synclaire was born January 8, 1998, by Cesarean Section. She was a perfectly healthy little girl weighing in at a *whopping* 5lbs, 10 ounces.   On that day, my life was forever changed.

"After Jordyn's birth, my relationship with ***The Respondent*** **became progressively worse. We did nothing but fight all the time. I was bitter, angry and hurt. I retreated to a dark place an emotional wasteland. I *wandered in the wilderness,* all alone."**

And now, I found myself with this beautiful baby girl who was looking to me to love, care, provide and protect her.

PROCESSING REJECTION & FILLING THE VOID

"Every time I thought I was being rejected from something good, I was actually being redirected to something better."
– Steve Maraboli

"It hurts, doesn't it? Giving someone everything you can think of. The wings to fly and roots to stay and yet watch them

choose none of those, leaving you hanging in the middle of void and nothingness."
-Akshay Vasu

"Rejection is a cold thing."

My views and unhealthy emotions about marriage and family rose to the surface. I resurrected the feelings of the same sad, broken and scared little black girl who just wanted to be loved. I didn't think I could do this alone. I tried to seek comfort and validation in all the wrong places, and all that did was leave me feeling emptier than ever.

During my whole life, I grew up fearing punishment from God. More than anything, I wanted to be comforted. So many things were happening that were out of my control that I felt I had nowhere to turn but to God. I didn't want the coldness of the Catholic Church. I wanted something warm. I needed to *meet* Jesus.

When we're hurting, it's not uncommon to look for ways to fill the void. The void is made up of the empty, lonely feelings that stem from holes in our heart and soul. Sometimes these holes are fresh wounds like a breakup, a death in the family, or a lost job. Sometimes they stem from something much deeper, like a lack of connection with family growing up, a childhood trauma, or hurt caused by someone in our past. My void was rejection.

When you lose something or someone, all of the wounds, emptiness, pain and hurt are exposed.

"As much as it hurts, the void should not be feared. The void is where miracles, strength and change are born."

What I knew for sure was that I would never get married again. I had too many bad experiences to even think about turning to a man again. I thought I detested marriage before, but the rejection I felt from *The Respondent* only made it worse.

I had to remember that whatever was going on in my life, that it was no longer just about me. I had a daughter that deserved only the best I could give her, including a real family. *The Respondent* and I lived together for two years. I finally gave in, and begrudgingly, we got married, Jordyn was now two years old.

THE DEFINITION OF INSANITY

"If you always do what you always did, you will always get what you always got."
-Albert Einstein

People often tell me that changing old ways seems too hard, or that they're too old to change.

"I believe nothing is more draining than trying to force a relationship into *happily ever after."*

Here is a bit of surprising news: Truth precedes love. Love doesn't hurt, and neither does a good marriage.

A year into our marriage, I had to face the fact that my marriage was a lie. The life I created was a lie. I thought I was done with facades. How could I have returned to my old ways? Now, my new truth

143

was that I should never have forced my will on someone else.

Here's another surprising fact: marriage will not improve your relationship.

"Marriage doesn't automatically *fix* what's wrong with your spouse. Marriage isn't going to make a cheater commit. Marriage isn't going to make a deadbeat get a job. Marriage won't make anyone smarter, funnier, more charming, more thoughtful, or more of anything you want them to be…"

except more married.

The warning signs were there, but I ignored them all. In my mind, I again did the right thing for the wrong reason. This time, it had to work. I decided to fight for my marriage and my family. I needed spiritual help. I joined a local church. My marriage was in freefall, and I needed Jesus! I went to my pastor for help. Surprisingly, the senior pastor told me flat out that he could not help us. I thought, "That's odd." I soon discovered that my church did not care about my marriage or me. The senior pastor assigned an elder and his wife who had been married for 38 years to help us work through our problems. What I later realized was that this leader was trying to help himself to me!

He had no intentions of helping us with our problems. Looking back on the whole experience, I wish that we had had a safe place to go to receive godly counsel before our marriage fell apart.

Divorce is never easy, but it's one of those life events that deserve a serious postmortem examination to figure out what really happened. My marriage was dead on arrival – DOA! When my divorce was final, I learned a lot about what it takes to make a relationship work.

We tend to learn best from failure. According to Bishop Dale Bronner, "First, failures are normal and inevitable. Second, failure is the womb of success. It's the thing that births something new out of you."

When a marriage fails, you're certainly primed for a lot of learning and self-reflection. On the surface, my marriage had the makings of something that could have worked: no infidelity and no abuse (not physically anyway). If I'm perfectly honest, we sucked at dealing with issues. Jordyn was four when *The Respondent* and I divorced. By this time, it was all about me.

CHAPTER TEN:

PULLED ASIDE FOR A DATE WITH DESTINY

"Letting go means to come to the realization that some people are a part of your history, but not a part of your destiny."

-Steve Maraboli

Ending relationships is hard. It is normal to have feelings of grief, sadness, anger, and fear. We all enjoy the comfort of retrospection. We know how everything turns out because we've lived through it. My new reality was I am a divorced, Christian woman.

"Divorce is like having a giant paper cut on your soul."

I never planned to get a divorce. I don't believe I ever thought, "Well, if it doesn't work out I can always *jump ship*." I married with the intention of making it work. I'm not a failure, and I never give up!

147

I must admit I didn't treat my marriage like God intended for me to treat it. I didn't live my life as a whole like He would want for me. Though I never wanted the divorce, in retrospect, I'm not surprised things fell apart. I was different then; ignorant, insecure and impatient.

After my divorce, I reassessed where I was on the landscape of my dreams. I had a great job making good money. I had a plan to retire in ten years. My daughter was growing up so fast. My marriage to my career was flourishing, and that's all I knew, which was just the way I wanted it.

Looking over my accomplishments, I managed to stack up some *wins*. I received not one, but two degrees: a Bachelor of Science degree in Health Care Supervision and a Master's degree in Business Administration - Technology Management. I even managed to earn my Project Management credential and became a certified Project Management Professional (PMP). I was convinced that I was finally living my dream, but something was missing. I couldn't rest. I realized that missing component was *peace of mind*.

I restored my relationship with God, and I put my focus on Him, raising my daughter and work. I wanted to find some rest from the insanity that had once again become my life.

How was I ever going to find peace of mind? One way was to look for the beginning in every ending. A wise man once said, "Every new beginning comes from some other beginning's end." I said to myself,

"Dear Past, thank you for all the life lessons you have taught me. Dear Future, I am ready now!"

A great beginning always occurs at the exact moment you thought would be the end of everything.

Most people would define peace of mind as the absence of mental stress and anxiety. The expression *peace of mind* conjures up images of Buddha-like composure, wherein calm, comfort, and tranquility are so prevalent nothing can disturb the one who has peace of mind.

I realized you experience a peaceful mind and heart after you recognize, God, the all-wise and loving Father, has a purpose in our trials. "We know that all things work together for good to those who love God and are called according to His purpose." (Romans 8:28) (NIV)

The Bible says in Philippians 4:6-7, "Be anxious for nothing, but in everything, by prayer and petition, with thanksgiving, present your requests to God. And the peace of God, which surpasses all understanding, will guard your hearts and minds in Christ Jesus." (NIV)

Admittedly, many people wait until times get really rough before they turn to God. With God involved in our lives, we can rest easy. As we get to know God and listen to what he says in the Bible, he brings about that peace of mind in our lives, because we know him. We see life from his vantage point, aware of his faithfulness and ability to take care of us.

So, no matter what the future holds, we can place our hope in God as our constant. He's waiting to prove himself in our lives if we will turn to him and seek him.

God did this for me, and...

"I found peace of mind -- a currency worth more than gold."

Renewed, I started attending another church that filled me with hope. Unbeknownst to me, I was about to be pulled over for a date with destiny.

I changed my priorities to accomplish tasks that served God. The Bible says in 1 Peter 4:10-11, "As each has received a gift, use it to serve one another, as good stewards of God's varied grace: whoever speaks, as one who speaks oracles of God; whoever serves, as one who serves by the strength that God supplies—in order that in everything God may be glorified."(NKJ)

I like helping people, so I began to volunteer at my new church. My first assignment was working at the information counter, which was a natural fit. I invested my time in volunteering and wanted to serve in any way that I could.

I also loved being a mom, which was my highest calling, a distinct honor, and privilege. I still can't believe God saw me *fit for duty*. My daughter was a constant source of joy and fulfillment. I was in awe watching her grow up. My cocker spaniel, Princess was the best *boyfriend* I've ever had. Everything was in balance and life was good. I was finally living my dream, or so I thought.

I think sometimes we like to let God know when His work is done. I knew I was changing for the better, and already I had formulated plans on how everything else would fall into place.

God loves you so much and has a good plan for your life. Even if you are in the middle of a disaster right now, don't give up hope. I know what He's done for me; bringing restoration to every part of my life, He'll do the same for you!

"I think peace of mind is a bit like gourmet, organic, homemade chicken noodle soup. Once you've had it, the other stuff just won't do. If you've made it yourself, that's even better."

FINE, FAST & FORTY

"And what is better than wisdom? Woman. And what is better than a good Woman? Nothing."
– *Chaucer*

It is inevitable that as you grow older your tastes change, new experiences and influences coupled with the march of time, mean that you evolve from who you were to the person you want to become.

Transformation coach, Connie Chapman expressed it this way, "The first thing to get clear on, is that becoming the person you want to be is not an outside search. You will not find your self-love in the affection you get from other people. You will not find your confidence in the title you hold at work. You will not find your true abundance of money in your bank account. The qualities that you wish to embody need to be created from the inside out."

Women begin to go through many subtle physical changes when they turn 40. I was no different. After 39 years of not being 40, I decided to give it a try. Maturity brings with it responsibility. With responsibility comes sensibility. Sensibility leads to confidence. My confidence had vastly improved. My tastes were changing. Things that appealed to me in the past no longer had appeal.

As I was climbing the ladder of success, my apartments reflected my tastes of the time; they were decked out with the trendiest furniture and accessories. My bedrooms were filled with black lacquer and brass furniture. Bad taste never looked so good.

After I had purchased a new home, it was important for my home to reflect an older, bolder me. There's nothing more powerful than getting a picture of your future that will cause you to be pregnant with purpose and give birth to action. I needed a living space that was more representative of the woman I'd become. No more black lacquer.

Ethan Allen, here I come! I hired an interior designer and completely overhauled my home, furniture, window treatments, and accessories. I created an environment where my home would rise to meet me. I filled my new sanctuary with furnishings that would withstand the tests of time and taste. This renovation caused me to feel empowered, focused and more at peace.

"I felt balance. Balance is a sign of maturity."

This new level of maturity led me to realize the secret in becoming all you want to be, lies in remembering you are already everything you want to be. Everything you desire is already inside of you. All the resources you need to create it are inside of you too. What you are looking for is not *out there* in the world that you see.

If your level of self-love, confidence or abundance is dependent on circumstances that are external to you, then you will live in constant fear of them being taken away. Real inner power comes from believing that the source of all you desire to become, is within you. Being 40 is awesome! *Reinventing* my life put me on a course for a date with destiny. Enter, the *Game Changer Guy*!

155

The Game Changer Guy!

To the world, you may just be one person, but to one person you may be the world."
– Mother Theresa

I'm free! I mean I'm really free! Free to exhale, free to be myself, free to do the things that bring me joy. My emotional compass was set to freedom. I wasn't anxious about anything. I finally figured out what I wanted to do with my life and I was well on my way. I built my career and a new home. I was a single mother raising an awesome daughter. I had a healthy relationship with myself. I reconnected to the Source of my supply, the Source of my life and the Source of love. I love the woman I've become. No more tricks, manipulations, or lies. I am free! I'm living my dream, or so I thought.

"It happens when you least expect it; I'm speaking about relationships -- that's what they say anyway. On the other hand, if you are open and willing to make yourself vulnerable without

putting expectations on how or when you'll have a relationship, then the universe will work hard to send it to you."

If you have placed too much negative attention on a relationship (i.e. why isn't it happening or I have such bad luck with dating) then it can't happen.

If you feel entitled to meeting someone, but you are not doing the work on yourself, it can't happen. If you are so busy working that your *cab light is not on*, (like I was), then it can't happen.

If you are grounded in who you are and move towards the life you want to have with a potential spouse; it will happen faster. If you are ready, you will just walk out your door and boom! He'll be there! This is The Law of Attraction.

"Meeting *the one* doesn't always look like a romantic comedy. Trust me, I know. I wasn't looking or praying to have a man in my life. Ironically, I met my husband when he was married to someone else."

Stop! I hear you judging me! Don't jump to conclusions. We didn't have a salacious affair. There was no unrequited love. On the contrary, I was friends with both he and his wife. Let me explain.

One Sunday, almost 12 years ago, I was visiting a church with some friends. Elder Derek intercepted our entourage and offered to give us a tour. During the tour, we talked about our professions. Ironically, we both worked in the information technology field, me in the federal sector and he in the private sector.

Derek inquired about a position at the agency where I worked, and we happily exchanged business cards. I told him I would keep him updated if any positions came available. Truth be told, I never followed up with him and threw his card in the garbage.

Four years passed and I finally joined the church I had visited many times in the past. One Sunday, during a business fair at the church, I met Sandy. She was spirited, smart, energetic and feisty. She was also a Mary Kay representative. We talked about makeup, lipstick, and other *girl stuff*. We connected on so many levels.

During our conversation, she stated, "I think my husband knows you." I answered, "Who's your husband?" Sandy responded, "His name is Derek, and he is in the café." When I looked up, to my surprise, it was the same gentleman who had given my friends and I a tour of the church a few years ago. I was completely shocked that they both remembered me. We became a family of friends. This was another divine appointment.

Fast forward, one year later, Sandy became gravely ill and passed away the following year. When a friend loses a loved one, your heartaches for them. I wanted so much to comfort, soothe and make things better, for Derek and his daughter Jasmine. Derek's daughter was only 18 years old at the time of her mother's passing. She had just begun her freshman year in college. My heart bled for them both.

"I wanted anxiously to help alleviate their pain. I knew after the flowers had faded and

159

the sympathy cards had all been packed away, what Derek and Jasmine needed most were friends. Faithful friends who would be available and willing to be on hand. I was a faithful friend."

Derek and Jasmine left Arizona and returned home to Florida. They were gone for over six weeks. I knew he needed time to begin healing. The rumors swirling around the church were that Derek was not coming back to Arizona because *there was nothing left for him here.* We lost touch, and I didn't call Derek during this time because I knew he needed time and space.

Seven or so weeks later, Derek walked back into the church. I think everyone was shocked because no one expected him to return. He found me at the information counter, and we caught up. He told me that he and Jasmine were doing better and that being around family certainly helped to put them on the road to healing. I was glad to see his bright smiling face, looking like the friend I hadn't seen in over seven weeks. I could tell he was alright.

160

After the dust had settled and Derek re-engaged his life in Arizona, we began to hang out as friends. We would grab lunch or a gelato after church, or on Saturday's, Derek would come to Jordyn's soccer games.

We hung out when we could for about a year. In my mind, it was nice to have a friend to spend time with -- someone who didn't have an agenda. No pressure, no problem! The added benefit was my *peace of mind* remained solidly intact, because there was no chance anything more could happen.

LEARNING TO TRUST

"The best way to find out if you can trust somebody is to trust them."

-Ernest Hemingway

My broken marriage left me determined never to need or trust anyone again. In love and in life, our vulnerability is one of our greatest strengths. We often believe we risk too much by being vulnerable; in fact, the opposite is true. When we build a wall around us to protect ourselves from our big, bad fears, we miss out on so much.

"I think in the back of my mind, I somehow processed fears that had laid dormant. My biggest fear was believing I was unworthy of love, or that I could not recognize real love when it was not edged with lies and deception."

When we live with the mindset that something may be taken away from us (physically or emotionally), or that we need to be in control of everything that happens, we endure fear on a daily basis. It's exhausting to live this way. It will make you cynical, suspicious, and unable to follow your heart because we are afraid of what might happen.

Vulnerability has never been my strong suit. It's no wonder, to be vulnerable, you must be okay with all of you. That's the thing about vulnerability that no one tells you about. Being vulnerable is not just about showing the parts of you that are shiny, beautiful, and fun. It's about revealing what you deny or keep hidden from other people. We all do this to some extent. You've got to love everything about yourself if you want to be vulnerable.

"Most of us have probably experienced vulnerability through default. More often than not, we are either forced into that state through conflict, or we are surprised by it after our circumstances feel more comfortable. Few of us consciously choose vulnerability. Why? Because the stakes are too high."

If we reveal our authentic selves, there is the great possibility that we will be misunderstood, labeled, or worst of all, rejected. The fear of rejection can be so powerful that some wear it like armor. My first experience with vulnerability came when I *met* Derek.

You may be asking yourself, "I thought she said she met Derek some time ago?" Well, I was introduced to him some years ago, but it wasn't until after our relationship deepened that I actually *met* him.

163

In the land of *peace of mind*, my house was a fortress with fortified walls I constructed to protect me from pain. These walls resembled every fear I ever had: rejection, ridicule, failure, being wronged, and being taken advantage of. Nobody likes to feel exposed, but if you are someone who suffered at the hands of betrayal and trust issues, your fears become even more magnified.

Learning to be vulnerable after deep pain can feel impossible, but it doesn't have to be. If you consciously *choose* to stay open and trust, you will find your world changes for the better in ways you never imagined.

Of course, it is always right to use our instincts as our guide. You should never set yourself up to be shot down emotionally by someone who doesn't deserve your trust. At the same time, you should not let negative past experiences allow you to believe it's not safe to trust again. I know, because this happened to me, I learned how to trust.

ARE YOU READY FOR A NEW RELATIONSHIP?

"The greatest relationships are the ones you never expected to be in."

–Debra Williamson

"I think you need to fall in love with the wrong person. I think you need to cry, sweat, bleed and fail. I think you need to have bad relationships and bad breakups. I think you need all of that so that when the right person comes along, you can sigh with relief and say, *"Ah yes, this is how it is supposed to feel."***"**

You know when something feels right. In relationships, there is that chemistry; that electricity that gets you excited. Pay attention to that. Your best decision-making strategy will be to use both facts and feelings. This is the best advice I ever gave myself. I wish I had taken it!

Months and months went by and Derek and I spent a lot of time together, not romantically, but in a way, that fulfilled a need we both had. Neither of us wanted to be in isolation.

165

Divine appointments always happen to me when I least expect. One Sunday, as I was volunteering at church Derek found me in the bookstore. His nervous energy was funny. He started rambling incoherently about friends telling him that he should go out. He continued his word-ball by saying he should do more than just sweep his pool every day and play golf.

Derek continued, "I wonder if Deb would be interested in going to the movies with me." The fact that he was looking at me and speaking to me in the third person was hilarious. I stopped him dead in his tracks because I could sense his nervousness. I told him, "Of course Derek, we are friends. I would be happy to go to the movies with you anytime." I had no idea that this was his attempt to ask me out on a *real date*. I think my response was a bit embarrassing for him.

A week or two passed when I received a call from Derek. He started the conversation by asking me what type of food I liked. I told him I was mainstream with my tastes: chicken fingers, buffalo chicken wings, French fries, salad, corn on the cob,

166

the usual. He then asked me out to dinner. He told me he wanted to take me somewhere *special.* I said, "Of course, I'd love to."

In the meantime, I had some friends visiting from California who were in town for a conference that weekend. I invited them to come to dinner with us not realizing this was Derek's attempt to have an official date with me. He made a reservation for us at Trader Vic's at the Valley Ho Hotel, in Scottsdale, AZ. His intention was to introduce me to a new dining experience.

Before we arrived at the restaurant, my friends told me how hungry they were. However, they were not prepared to eat at a high-end restaurant. I guess they thought we were going to Applebee's. The look on their faces as they scanned the menu was too funny. After looking over the menu, they decided to share a plate of fried rice. The only beverage they had was water. When it came time to order dessert, they quipped, "The best cheesecake we ever had was at Jack-In-The-Box!" We're going to save our appetite for that.

That evening was epically funny! I think Derek was mortified. He may have thought the *Clampetts* ruined the mood and the ambiance he tried hard to create.

"When dinner was over, I invited Derek over to my house to hang out with my friends. He respectfully declined."

I still did not connect the dots. I had no idea Derek's interests in me had changed.

Some weeks had passed since Derek, and I spoke after that historically funny dinner. I thought that was odd, but I wasn't necessarily alarmed because I was unaware of the fact that he wanted to take our relationship to a new level.

When he finally called, I was happy to hear from him. He confided in me that he was disappointed that the dinner he planned didn't turn out the way he expected. I was shocked. I had no idea. I apologized. I felt horrible. At that moment, the cab light came on! Derek wanted to spend time with me to cultivate a relationship beyond friendship. Was I ready for that?

To get to a place where you are comfortable being vulnerable and trust a person or situation, you must first be honest with yourself.

"Once we look the big bad fears in the eye and see they are trying to protect us from being hurt, we can respond by saying, *"Thanks, but no thanks. I'd like to see what's beyond that wall.""*

Once your heart says, "Yes," beware of monumental challenges that may come your way. This is the point! Love brings our fears (feelings such as doubt, rejection, jealousy, anger, frustration, and confusion) forward so we can set them right. I could finally tell Derek I was ready to look beyond that wall. I was ready to trust. I was ready to explore. I was ready to be vulnerable.

Eighteen months prior, I would have been too scared to read the lesson in church. Gradually, I was encouraged, loved, coaxed and convinced back into

169

self-belief; never my strong suit. Slowly, my life was being changed by the *Game Changer Guy*.

CHAPTER ELEVEN:

WHEN IN DOUBT

When in doubt, don't!

-Benjamin Franklin

Derek is a man of integrity and honesty. Derek is **well respected**, fun, smart, adventurous and trustworthy. He is a man of influence, a leader, confidant, trendsetter, daredevil, and he lives life to its fullest capacity. Derek likes to talk; ask anybody. Derek likes to talk! His character also follows his anointing. He loves photography, and he's always snapping pictures. Me, I hate having my picture taken. Derek is *so* different from me.

He photographed me all the time; he had us photographed together; he took pictures everywhere we went. He is emotionally openhearted and generous.

"I learned to lean on his unfailing kindness and his chirpy, energetic optimism. His touching attitude that no day is too long, no

potential adventure too far away to be worth attempting, contrasted sharply with my fundamental distrust of enthusiasm."

My languid response to all excursions was, "What on earth for?" But then I'd go anyway, and rarely regretted it.

Derek was always seeking adventure at every turn, corner, and intersection.

Derek loved his church. Except for his blood family, nothing was more important to him than his church family. He was a leader at his church, and he loved to serve. I never had the heart for a leadership role in church. I was not called to ministry. I felt most comfortable helping behind the scenes. After my previous experience being wounded by church members, I came to believe most church pastors were hypocrites.

As I let my guard down and chose to trust this honorable man, our relationship began to flourish, but I still had doubts. Not in him per se, but in myself. I wasn't good enough for this pillar in the church, this man of God, this man of principle and integrity. Why in the world would he want to *hitch his star to my wagon?*

Every insecurity I thought I resolved, rushed to the surface. I told Derek we could not possibly have a serious, romantic relationship because I would not be accepted in his world. I told him if he pursued our relationship, everyone at the church would go to hell— that's how I felt. I was not deserving of a godly man. I would bring him down. I couldn't receive love because I didn't know how to give love.

To add insult to injury, Derek grew up in a stable home. His parents have been married for over fifty years. His sister was married to a physician. Derek's entire family tree was stable. I would never fit into his world.

My past was checkered— I came from a broken home, stability was not my experience. A relationship with me would only sully his reputation. Nevertheless, Derek would not take *no* for an answer. This was difficult and scary for me. I asked myself,

"How many pieces of your heart can you lose and still retain the ability to deeply and fully love?"

The answer was not as much as I thought, because the more break ups, the more scars, the harder it is to open up next time. How ironic, our culture is always drawn to watch great love stories, but often we are too cowardly to write ourselves into the script.

The question for me was, did I have the courage to open my heart to love? Was I really ready?

GROWING UP FOR REAL!

"Maturity comes when you stop making excuses and start making changes."
-Anonymous

Mature couples don't *fall in love* they step into it. Love isn't something you fall into; it's something you rise up for. Falling denotes lowering oneself, dropping down and being stuck somewhere lower than where you started. You must get up from a fall. Love isn't like that— at least not with people who are doing it right.

"Immature couples fall; mature couples coast. Because love is either a passing game or it's forever. Love is either wrong, or it's right. A couple is either mature or immature."

Derek and I have always enjoyed a very transparent relationship. He is the only man I ever felt safe with sharing my deepest thoughts and feelings. Derek has never lied to me, not once. He was too good to be true.

On January 9, 2008, one day after my daughter's 10th birthday, Derek and I were sitting at my kitchen table. We were talking about my past, and I was sharing my heart with him about past hurts, failed relationships and how much I treasured being a mother. I became very emotional, and tears were streaming from my eyes when Derek blurted out, "Deb, I love you!" I nearly fainted. I thought I was hallucinating. I was stunned into silence. He could tell I was in shock.

Derek then rose out of his seat and picked up a piece of paper and wrote the following: "Debra Lynn Hodges, I declare this ninth day of January in the year 2008, I Love You! Signed, Derek T. Williamson." I was blown away. This could not be happening. To this day, I still have that hand-written piece of paper.

Was I mature enough to embark on another relationship with a man who claimed to love me? Immature relationships ask questions; mature relationships answer them.

"Immature relationships are all about doubts. Does he love me? Is he cheating on me? Will we be together in two months?"

I raised doubts. Doubts tend to surface in relationships when things progress in a new direction.

Mature couples don't need to ask questions. They already know the answers, and they don't need reassurance from their partners. They are comfortable and secure and free of doubt because mature love isn't about all those small questions, but a comfort in knowing the big question is answered.

As we settled into our newly defined relationship, my insecurities were resurrected. I found myself questioning Derek's motives. One evening Derek came over for a visit after leaving a meeting. I was so paranoid that when he leaned in to kiss me, I pulled him close so that I could smell him. I know how weird this sounds but I needed to make sure he didn't smell like the little soap you get at hotels.

If he did, that would mean he had a booty call and showered before coming over. Sounds crazy, doesn't it? Who does that? I did! But's that what you do when you're not healed from old wounds. You act irrationally. You become unhinged.

Here is a man who enjoyed twenty-one years of wedded bliss; now he's hooked up with *cray-cray*! The look on Derek's face was priceless. He couldn't fathom how any woman would be in a relationship with a man she couldn't trust. How could I still have trust issues? *Debra, please grow up for real!*

CHAPTER TWELVE:

HAPPILY, EVER AFTER...FOR REAL THIS TIME!

"There are two things you can do with your past; you can run from it, or you can learn from it."

-Rifiki

After Derek's wife passed away, it was open season on him, literally. The *tabernacle hoes* came out of the woodwork. Women were *throwing themselves at him left and right,* especially those *thirsty* women at church. If you're not careful, the church can be a breeding ground for thirsty women, because there is something sexy about the Holy Spirit. Women are drawn to the power they think a man of God holds.

One woman was so bold that she went to Derek's parent's home and pronounced she was going to be the next 'Mrs. Derek Williamson.'

Women from his hometown were mailing him their panties via Fed Ex services and sending lewd photos to his phone. Poor thing! He was like a *deer caught in the headlights.* He was so out of his depth that he didn't have any experience with this predatory behavior. He asked me how he should handle this and I told him to be firm and let these women know their advances were unwelcomed. To top it off, he'd fallen in love with a woman who was still harboring signs of brokenness.

"Immature relationships judge you on your past. Mature relationships help you carry it."

We all have a past, and in many cases, it consists of one we are not proud of. Mature couples don't just accept one another's past, but want to help heal the wounds. They look beyond the mistakes and the flaws and see the beauty in the future together.

I'm so grateful Derek was mature, and because of his love for me, I found that I no longer behaved in an immature way.

THE AMBUSH!

"Love is an irresistible desire to be irresistibly desired."
-Robert Frost

September 12, 2008, my day started out routinely with one exception, it was my birthday. The night before Derek left to go home, he strategically left gifts for me around my house, in my office, in my car, in my kitchen. Mid-morning Derek called to wish me happy birthday. He told me after he got off work, he and Jordyn were taking me out to dinner. I was overjoyed. All day I looked forward to seeing Derek and having a quiet celebration. We arrived at the restaurant. As the hostess was taking us to our table, to my surprise, Derek had invited some of my friends to join us in my birthday celebration. I was deeply touched.

"I thought, *I have the most thoughtful and considerate boyfriend ever.*"

My friend Lisa was there. She asked me to cut the cake and blow out the candles before we ordered our food. I thought it strange, but I went along. Just as I finished blowing out the candles, Derek tapped me on my shoulder. He was behind me on bended knee. As I turned toward him, I noticed he had a candle pinched between his fingers. Placed on top of the candle was the most beautiful ring I'd ever seen. Derek softly said, "Sweetheart, you forgot to blow out this one! Debra, will you marry me?" "What?" I panicked. I crawled under the table and began to scream before I knew it; an ugly cry ran like a river. This went on for almost 10 minutes.

My friends were screaming, "Debra, get out from under the table. You haven't given him an answer and the candle is burning his finger!" I couldn't catch my breath. I couldn't believe this was happening. How was it possible this wounded and scarred little black girl from the Southside of Chicago, had a *king* ask her for her hand in marriage? After I had composed myself, I shouted,

"YES!" Was *this* the dream I was supposed to be living?

I must have had a *wholesale brain fart*! How could I have said yes? Have my views on marriage changed? I thought I hated marriage? Is this what happens when you embrace life? One thing I knew for sure, I needed to take a risk, get out of my comfort zone, stretch my muscles, and say *yes* to life. Derek was worth the risk.

But was I ready to transition from being a woman to being a wife again? Derek was determined we were going to be prepared for marriage. I strongly agreed. We sunk our teeth into all things marriage related, for we had an unquenchable appetite. We attended pre-marital seminars and together we began serving in the marriage ministry at church.

"I was overwhelmed with what I was learning. You mean to tell me all I had to do was find the truth about marriage in the Bible?"

Where was all this information on how to have a godly marriage during my failed marriages? Why wasn't I better prepared?

Taking in all this information was overwhelming. I felt as though I was a toddler learning how to walk. Then something miraculous happened. I found myself drawn in and wanting to better understand God's design, plan, and purpose for marriage. I was all-in.

The more I learned, the more I realized how badly distorted my views were on marriage. I felt guilty. Then I had feelings of anger. The churches I previously attended never taught at this depth on the topic of marriage. As I began to understand the spiritual implications of divorce, I wanted to run to the first confessional booth I could find, to confess and repent! If I had only known. I would have made better choices. I finally realized that I could have my happily ever after, after all!

UNLACING MY TRACK SHOES

"You can give without loving, but you can never love without giving." -Victor Hugo, Les Miserables

Here's the scenario: Now, I am a late-40 something professional, hard-working woman. I have a 10-year-old daughter, and I have been single for about five years by choice and I decided to finally put my needs first, work on my career, and to nurture my relationships with friends and family. I had no intentions of entering a relationship because the man I wanted did not exist. He hadn't been born yet! I found my self-confidence again, and I knew my worth. I was done with compromise. I would never abandon my peace of mind but I just said yes to Derek. How could this be?

After news of our engagement sunk in, I had to come to the stark realization that I agreed to marry this AMAZING man. He was more than I could have possibly dreamed for — you know, too good to be true! He was good *to me* and *for me*. We fit. He was loyal and a man of integrity.

"So why would a woman run away from everything she says she wants and has finally been given?"

I wanted to stay in our relationship, but every day I had to talk myself into not breaking it off with him. EVERY DAY. The anxiety I was suffering from was stifling. Why am I trying to sabotage this good thing by running away? Was this kind of anxiety normal?

Derek picked up on this behavior from the beginning of our engagement, actually, from the beginning of our courtship. Good relationships often freak us out more than mediocre ones. The reason most people run from healthy relationships is because they have not found 'self-love.'

It's impossible to be in a healthy romantic relationship if you don't love yourself. When a person lacks self-love, they lack self-worth, self-confidence, and happiness. They don't believe they are worthy of the love of someone else, so it becomes impossible to find it. This could not be me, I found self-love, or so I thought.

185

"Now, if you resemble this, understand that obtaining self-love isn't difficult. It takes a conscious choice to live a life you are proud to live."

Are you a good parent? Are you doing what you love professionally? Are you proud of your career? Do you like the way you treat others? Do you value the way you live your life and the decisions you make? If you can say yes to these, you have a better chance of finding love.

I was confident I had self-love; it took me a lifetime to find it, so why the inclination to run? I think the answer was the more I wanted someone; the greater the possibility of that someone rejecting me scared me away. If we are unable to look at ourselves and be honest about our pain and how that fuels our behavior, we will keep repeating the same patterns.

I don't know about you, but that got old for me, and I had to own my fear of rejection to untangle myself from this pattern. I am glad I did. Now I feel like an adult most of the time, instead of like a scared little girl who fears rejection. This has made a world of difference for me, and it could for you as well.

Derek was so patient with me. He would give me daily *don't run* pep talks. Derek would say, "Baby, unlace and take off your track shoes. I'm not going anywhere!" Derek was my first experience in a healthy relationship. Our relationship was not perfect, but it was healthy. It felt good. The fact that I could be my true self was refreshing.

I'm with a man who respects and honors me, and who I respect and honor. I trained myself to be happy. I unlaced my track shoes, and Derek and I entered into covenant on November 8, 2008, in a clandestine ceremony attended by only a handful of family & friends. We decided to have a second ceremony at dusk, on the shores of the Caribbean Sea in St. Lucia. The second ceremony took place December 15, 2008. Needless to say, 2008 was life changing for both of us.

THE BREAK. THE BOND. THE BLEND.

"The ultimate purpose of marriage is not to make us happy, but to glorify God."
-Nancy Lee DeMoss

"Marriage is hard." I heard that statement all my life, and I lived out that statement at different points in my life. Marriage can be incredibly difficult, no matter how great the guy or gal is or how prepared you think you are.

"It takes a lot to meld two lives, two different personalities, from two different backgrounds, equipped with two entirely different ways of dealing with conflict and seeing the world."

Marrying Derek made sense logically, emotionally and spiritually. We did everything together. He had become the true North of my life. Most importantly, we served in the body of Christ together. We wanted our marriage to stand for something. However, what *I* didn't know about

188

having a godly marriage could have filled up a football arena!

Blending two lives is not as easy as one might think. This *till death do us part* stuff was becoming increasingly difficult. Do you have any idea how hard it is for a woman with a career, education, money, and independence to submit to a man, even if that man was Derek Williamson?

"I didn't fully understand what a *helpmate* was or the importance of submitting to my husband. Even though we did all the premarital counseling and seminars, nothing is like actually being called to take what you've learned and put it to practice."

I was still in need of a wholesale brainwashing. I had to unlearn behaviors I knew didn't work and learn new behaviors that would produce results that would bring God glory.

However, everything for me this time around was profoundly different. Derek and I agreed at the very beginning that divorce was **NOT** an option

189

and we took it off the table. Our marriage would last. Our marriage would weather any storm. Our marriage would be all that God designed it to be.

The Bible says that wisdom is the principal thing, but in all thy getting, get understanding. I had to go back to the basics and gain a fundamental understanding of what God intended for marriage.

The Bible says that in the beginning, after God created all the things upon the earth, including Adam, He said,"It is not good that man should be alone; I will make him a helper comparable to him"(Genesis 2:18) (NIV). God then created the woman and presented her to Adam. Then Scripture declares this timeless principle: "Therefore a man shall leave his father and mother and be joined to his wife, and they shall become one flesh." (Genesis 2:24). Within this passage, God reveals His intention that a man and his wife are to become one flesh.

"Oneness is God's ultimate purpose and goal for every marriage. Oneness in marriage is biblical. It is not about our happiness in marriage; it's about God's calling and purpose."

190

When it comes to marriage, many Christians believe if they go to a good church, take a marriage enrichment course and occasionally read marriage books, they will have a strong marriage. Although these things are true and helpful, Derek and I learned you must be intentional when it comes to marriage.

I'm not going to lie, it was extremely hard at first for me to break from my old life, bond with my husband and blend our lives into one flesh. I began to understand the way God designed man and woman was to be complementary. Women are different from men, and we each have a specific design, purpose, and need.

I had to change my priorities and even tell my daughter that she no longer was first in my life. That conversation was necessary if I was serious about God's design for *right order* in marriage.

I also had to have the right people in my life to make this happen. I needed a different sphere of influence if I was ever going to be successful at this *marriage* thing!

191

THE RIGHT PEOPLE AT THE RIGHT TIME!

"God's answer to every problem is always a person."
-Bishop Dale Bronner

People precipitate change. On every level of life, we need others to introduce us to new relationships and opportunities and connections. One thing I know is that you should never discount the people God brings into your life. They might be the greatest gift of God to link you to your healing, to your deliverance, and to your growth and development. God placed us in an environment that allowed this to happen.

Derek has always been keen on personal development and growth. He lives for seminars and conferences that teach about positive, permanent shifts in the quality of your life. He introduced me to one conference that would forever put us on a course we never saw coming. It was at the National Association of Marriage Enhancement (NAME)

International Marriage Conference (IMC) where we met Dr. Leo and Molly Godzich, founders of this worldwide, international ministry.

This divine appointment put us on a date with our destiny. This is where we were first introduced to what a marriage ministry looked like. At that conference, we learned that NAME had launched more than 200 counseling centers in 10 countries. There were over 2,000 people in attendance at that year's conference. The guest speakers were mind-blowing. I had never seen that many people assembled at one time all on fire for marriage. It was mesmerizing. The atmosphere was electric.

It was at this conference our passion was ignited to take up the mantle for marriage and work to help build marriages for the glory of God.

"As we found our passion, our marriage found its purpose."

Passion is a God-given desire that compels us to make a difference in our world. Our passion may be a dream, vision, burden or call. God gives each of us desires to move us to address the concerns of his heart. When we pursue our passion, or the concerns He places in our heart, we are focused and motivated. We feel alive, intense, and energetic.

Having a passion for ministry is hard work, and it doesn't equate to massive numbers of couples that want to sow into their relationships. Passion for marriage ministry produces a deep joy, which doesn't depend upon any denomination, title or church. This overwhelming sensation is all about being where God placed you and experiencing the joy of walking in obedience to Him.

Deep passion doesn't mean you don't face tough seasons. I've come to realize the more you want to do for the Lord, the greater the giants you'll face. We knew what we could not cause to happen on our own, God would cause us to accomplish. We knew it would be bigger than we could ever think. It would happen quicker than we imagined, and it would be more rewarding than we ever dreamed possible. Suddenly, a dream comes to pass. Suddenly, a promise is fulfilled. Suddenly, doors are opened.

"It is my belief that once you know your passion, you will know your calling. Everything you do in your external world begins in your internal world. Allow yourself to dream and dream *big.*"

February 3, 2013, God gave us, *Unbreakable Marriage Ministries.*

Our dream, our passion and our desire is to minister, train, equip and mentor couples on how to have a marriage that tells the truth about God. The dream God has birthed in us is to plant marriage ministries across the globe.

It's easy to decide how you want things to go, but all we need to do is move to the side and give God room to work. We need to change our wants so they fit within His will, rather than asking God to change His will to meet our wants.

There is a distinction between natural favor and supernatural favor. Natural favor must be earned, but supernatural favor is a gift. *Unbreakable Marriage Ministries* was a supernatural gift from God. What's ironic is the fact that I never had a heart for marriage and I most definitely did not want to serve in a marriage ministry. When I allowed the Holy Spirit to interrupt me, everything else simply fell into place. We, then, were able to begin laying the groundwork to build God's marriage ministry. The work God has called us to do has been impactful. We have seen marriages restored from the brink of divorce; separated couples not only reunited but are living in victory.

Derek and I not only have a marriage that is unbreakable, we have also been blessed with supernatural favor in that we are blessed to travel the globe and minister to couples about marriage without constraints. God has opened doors for us that no man can close. In the past year, we have traveled to three continents and six countries, and we're just getting started. This year we will open our international headquarters and continue the pursuit of the assignment we've been given to help heal broken marriages. My story is not finished; it's just beginning. My happily ever after is still being written.

CHAPTER THIRTEEN:

GOD-SIZED DREAMS

"One thing is that God-sized dreams have nothing to do with size. Maybe another way to think of it is God-shaped."

-Emily Freeman

A dreamer is defined as one who dreams, an idealist, a visionary; one who sees what is possible and believes that it can happen. When our focus becomes what we can do instead of what God will do, a sea of doubt and unbelief surrounds us.

The prophet Joel foretold of a time when God's Spirit would compel us to dream, "I will pour out my Spirit upon all people. Your sons and daughters will prophesy. Your old men will dream dreams, and your young men will see visions." (Acts 2:17, NLT)

If God lives in me, then the question becomes: what is the shape He has given for my dreams? If I don't know, maybe His dream for me is to be willing to find out.

When you have a God-given dream, your dream will outlive you, because it is that dream that will bring and bear fruit in the lives of other people.

God is a dream-giving God. God is the chief of all dreamers. So, finally, I get to answer the question "Am I living my dream? For me, the answer is hidden in the question. Let me explain. Living my God-sized dream had less to do with a *result* and more to do with a *process*. What I later discovered was this process was designed especially for me.

"This little black girl from the Southside of Chicago truly believes if I had accepted the good and bad parts of myself at a younger age, I would have avoided many of the wrong decisions I made in my life."

Once you know who you are inside, you begin to accept and love yourself fully. Once you truly love yourself from the inside, you can love and accept others, which provides a much higher probability of maintaining healthy relationships.

My mother used to say, "Water seeks its own level." Growing up, I never fully understood what she meant by this saying. Now I totally get it! We cannot live above the level of our thinking. You'll

198

never be in the future any more than what you can think you are right now. This is where the power to dream lives.

So, what's the point of my story? It's simple:

"From a young age, I felt insecure in my own skin. I was a highly sensitive child and, subsequently, struggled with low self-worth and low self-esteem for most of my life."

Although I had many friends and a good family, I consistently looked for approval outside of myself. I grew up believing the opinions of others were the only accurate representations of my core worth.

As a teenager, I witnessed the crumbling and eventual demise of my parents' marriage. During these years, I felt like an island. I was often plagued with a dark, mysterious unhappiness, which reflected, the standard teenage growing pains mixed with the trauma of losing my familial identity.

In a desperate attempt to counter these negative feelings, I sought the approval of men. When it was not provided, I felt like a failure. The truth was, I was far from being a failure. I had not learned to love me, not a fabricated me, the **real** me. At some point in my journey, I thought I was living my dreams. I discovered I was wrong.

God said apart from Him, we can't do anything and that all our dreams will be frustrated. The power, energy, and creativity needed to fulfill our dreams must flow from God.

"Every dream must pass the test of discouragement. Perhaps your roadblocks aren't roadblocks at all, but rather new beginnings in disguise. Perhaps your missteps are opportunities for growth, greater closeness with God or a nudge to take a leap of faith."

For a seed to sprout, the outer casing first has to fall away, or surrender, for new life to come. The same is true with our lives. We must let go a little — or sometimes a lot — for our fresh start to be revealed.

As Paul says in Philippians 3:13-14, "Forgetting what is behind and straining toward what is ahead, I press on toward the goal to win the prize for which God has called me heavenward in Christ Jesus." (NIV)

Whatever your passion, or what you enjoy in life, make sure you feed your soul with what inspires you. If you are not sure what your passion is, figure out who you are and what you want to become; your passion will spring forth from there.

The most common and most crucial question is, "How do I know which dreams in my heart are from God?" Here is the answer. You will know it's God's dream if:

1. It is bigger than you.

2. You can't let it go.

3. You would be willing to give up *your* dream in its place.

4. It will last forever.

5. It brings glory to God.

God hands us an extra-large vision *by design*. He is not just interested in what we accomplish for him, but in who we are becoming along the way. As we struggle to grow into what and who God calls us to do and be, we are changed and shaped more and more into the likeness of Christ.

My dream did not originate from me. It resided within me, but God is the one who put it there. He is the one that facilitated the birthing process. He is the source of your dreams.

"When people dream without God, the outcome can be hollow and unsatisfying."

Every person must come to God for his or her dream to make sense. In fact, without God, you might follow a dream for your life that God never put in your heart.

This is precisely what I did. I followed a dream that always landed me outside the perfect Will of God. When I accepted that God had a dream bigger than me, I stepped aside and allowed it to come to fruition. God-sized dreams give glory to Him, not us. God is up to something big when He plants His dreams in our hearts, and it's so much bigger than us. If we could achieve our calling in our own strength, we would readily take and receive the glory.

But when we stand at the base of an impossible mountain, shaking in our boots, knowing full well our legs could never carry us to the summit, we are forced to rely on God and praise him for every step he enables us to take along the way.

FOR SUCH A TIME AS THIS

"And who knows but that you have been created for such a time as this."
-Esther 4:14

I'm now at a new crossroads armed with time, grace and knowledge which has allowed me to make the right turn this time instead of the wrong one. Which then, of course, begs the question: "Was the first turn wrong when it taught me the lessons I needed to learn to make the RIGHT turn?"

"I think all turns are right turns because if they don't take us to the destination, they

prepare us for it. Every turn in my life brought me to this destination."

Today, Derek and I are both retired. He retired from AT&T in 2014 after thirty years of service, and I retired from the Department of Veterans in 2015 after thirty-seven years of federal service, at the top of my game.

When I think back to the start of my career, all those years ago as a GS-2 file clerk filing checks in numerical sequence to a position as a GS-14 project manager managing multi-million-dollar information technology projects, this is a full circle moment for me. My life put me in situations that almost defy explanation.

God had a much bigger dream for me. I finally gained consciousness about who I was to become. I was no longer just this little black girl from the South Side of Chicago. I am a woman of influence; a woman, other women look up to and seek out for counsel. I came to the realization I didn't need to try so hard; I just needed to be me.

Derek and I have been told our marriage is a model of transparency. One observer told us that we give people *access to their own humanity*. Another observer told us, "Ya'll a couple of bad mo'fos!" We're just doing the work and adhering to the process.

GOD'S DREAM IS ALWAYS BIGGER THAN US

"The first thing God does to build your faith is He gives you a dream. When God wants to work in your life, He'll always give you a dream—about yourself, about what He wants you to do, about how He's going to use your life to impact the world."
-Rick Warren

A God-sized dream, as Holley Gerth puts it: "It's not about what you do as much as how you do it. It's about pursuing life with passion and purpose and going with God wherever he leads. It's about not settling. It's about tenaciously believing you're made for more. Not as in 'bigger house, fancier car,

205

more luxurious lifestyle.' No, my friend, I mean 'more of Jesus, more of what He's created you to be, more of what he's called you to do.' Less of you, and more of all He is and all He has for you— which is beyond what you can even imagine."

God's dreams are always bigger than us! The Bible says in Revelation 3:8, "The Lord will open doors that no man can close and close doors that no man can open." One of the ways to know the Will of God is by open and closed doors, for where He guides, He always provides! Often this is how He gets us to do things: By closing some doors and opening others! God has opened doors for us to complete the work He has given us to enlarge the boundaries of His Kingdom.

My husband and I have founded one of the fastest growing marriage ministries in Arizona. Operating in our calling from God, we have counseled hundreds of couples teaching them how to solve their unsolvable marital problems. We have prepared a sizeable number of couples for the covenant of marriage. We have trained couples how to mentor other couples.

"When I think about how God is moving in our lives, causing us to accomplish the healing and restoration of marriage to build His kingdom, I'm reminded about my humble beginnings and my attitudes toward marriage. The Bible says God will take the foolish things of man and use them to confound the wise. I was his *foolish* thing."

Derek and I have been invited to teach about marriage at churches and other venues around the country. We've appeared on national television on the Trinity Broadcasting Network (TBN) speaking on marriage and family. Yes, this little black girl from the Southside of Chicago has appeared on TBN! I've written this book (that's huge), and there will be others to follow, on guess what? Marriage!

It took me a long time to realize the dreams I created for myself were not God's dreams for me because my dreams were way too small.

Finally, the bottom line: God will not allow any person to keep you from your destiny. They may be

207

bigger, stronger, or more powerful, but God knows how to shift things around and get you to where you're supposed to be.

"A life of pain and discouragement finally led me to this revelation: GOD SHAPED MY DREAMS long before I had any sense to understand what He was doing on my behalf."

Let Him shape yours.

That's the reality of God-sized dreams. Wise Solomon said, "There is nothing new under the sun." But he didn't say, "There is **no one new** under the sun." Every one of us is one-of-a-kind, and there will never be anyone else like us again. It doesn't matter if someone else has said it or done it already. *You haven't.* We need your version, perspective, and voice in this world. You're simply irreplaceable. A lifetime of learning and course correcting brought me to this revelation.

Allow the Holy Spirit to *interrupt* you; right where you are; especially if you think you are living your dreams. Had I said no, I couldn't imagine what would have happened to this little black girl from the Southside of Chicago.

Know this, the biggest reason you can't discover who you are is because you do not know Him. Once you know God, He will change You! What will you do with what you know? What will you do with what you possess? Will you allow God to birth in you a God-sized dream?

Lastly, remember what God has done for you so far. Look back and remind yourself how far He has brought you — and get excited all over again about what God is dreaming for you next; His God-sized dream!

DEBRA WILLIAMSON

ABOUT THE AUTHOR

Debra Williamson is the co-founder and Executive Director of Unbreakable Marriage Ministries. A Chicago native, Debra's roots go deep on the Southside. She grew up in Morgan Park and attended Holy Name of Mary elementary school on 112th and Loomis and Elizabeth Seton, H.S. in South Holland, IL.

Debra has an MBA in Technology Management, and she is a certified Project Management Professional (PMP). She recently retired from the federal sector after 37 years of distinguished service.

Debra and her husband, Derek, live and teach God's purpose, plan, and design for marriage. They have appeared on TBN International promoting the "Partner Gift of the Month" and on Arizona's TBN local show "Joy in Our Town."

Debra lives in Gilbert, Arizona with her husband. They have a blended family of 4 beautiful daughters and six grand-children. An unlikely union, Debra has a powerful testimony of what will happen when you allow the Holy Spirit to 'interrupt' you and change your BS (belief system)!

Made in the USA
San Bernardino, CA
10 August 2017